To Live and Love Well

The true story of a gay man's struggle
with poverty, abuse, and
excommunication from the
Mormon Church

WAYNE T. CHENEY

As told to Linda B. Myers

TO LIVE AND LOVE WELL

Wayne T. Cheney
As Told to Linda B. Myers

ABOUT THIS BOOK

To Live and Love Well is a true story; very few situations have been changed for dramatic emphasis. Characters and happenings are accurate. No part of this book may be used without written permission, except in the case of brief quotations in critical articles and reviews. The author of this book retains all rights except those expressly granted to Linda B. Myers and OlyPen Books. Email inquiries to Olypenauthors@olypen.com.

©2021 Wayne T. Cheney
Published by OlyPen Books
PO Box 312, Carlsborg, WA 98324
Cover design by Roslyn McFarland, Far Lands Publishing
Back Cover Photo: ©Glenda Hydler,
hydlerg@gmail.com
Interior design by Heidi Hansen

ISBN: 978-1736684115
For updates and chatter: Facebook.com/Wayne Cheney

Dedication

To John

My husband, my friend, my life

Contents

Preface

AUTHOR WAYNE T. CHENEY: You reach a time and age when remembrance and evaluation are essential. It may be to get in the last word, to leave a written history for others, to repair yourself through critical examination. Producing a reckoning of my life has been a goal of mine; it is the book you are holding in your hands.

My life has been turbulent, scarred by sorrow, blessed with talent. I am a gay man who grew up through dangerous years from extreme secrecy to hesitant acceptability. During those years, I faced severe poverty, heartbreaking losses, and excommunication from the Mormon Church for expressing my selfhood. At the same time, I have been blessed with wonderful children, countless friendships, and the lasting love of my spouse, John.

In these late years of my life, I can write that I have been successful in my goals. I live and love well. I accept who I am and what I was meant to be.

EDITOR LINDA B. MYERS: In the autumn of 2019, I received a call from a stranger. Wayne T. Cheney introduced himself as an artist who exhibited his oil paintings in a gallery where I sold my books. He was looking for an editor to help him with the stories of his life; the gallery owner recommended me.

The thing is that he hadn't written his story. I grumpily suggested he do that before seeking an editor. I gave him a few hints to get started, said goodbye, and immediately forgot Wayne T. Cheney. Frankly, in my experience, everyone has a story to tell, but few have the doggedness to actually do it.

In this case, I was wrong. Several months passed before he called again.

"I've written it," Wayne said.

Sure, I thought.

"I'll send it," he said.

Great, I thought, remembering all the times I'd heard people claim to have a rocking story to tell.

I was wrong again. By the end of the first page, I was hooked like a good-sized trout. As I skimmed through the story, I discovered a phoenix rising from the ashes of bitter poverty, an uncaring mother, a battle over the right to be gay. Wayne is a man put through Gay Aversion Therapy and excommunication by the Mormon Church, an artist capable of turning heads even on the Left Bank, a father of a beautiful family, a kind soul who finally found his "happily ever after" in his long marriage to John. Most of all, this is the story of becoming what you are meant to be in this world.

It has been an honor and privilege to work with Wayne. During the time of Covid-19, we've called and emailed back and forth. On rare occasion, we've met on the city pier in Port Angeles, WA to walk, laugh, and cry ... always behind masks. I have become an admirer; he has become my friend. One day, post-Covid, we hope to rip off the masks and smile.

1.

Life with Mama

I knew my mother was a whore before I knew what a whore was. I learned it the way other kids learn their mothers are teachers or florists or housewives. Whore is what people called her, although Verna was her real name.

That's one reason Gramma McComas took us away, but I was only three then, so what did I know? "Us" was my sister Jacquie and me. She was six to my three, and the font of all information in my life. Jacquie explained that Gramma wanted us raised right, to grow up Mormon. Gramma swooped us up from East Los Angeles and hauled us off to Utah where God's One True Church awaited us. The year was 1940.

Mama was five foot two, eyes of blue. My sister Jacquie was a beautiful study in browns. Coppery skin, chestnut eyes, dark chocolate hair. I was a blue-eyed towhead with skin so thin and fair it was irritated by almost everything. You see the problem here with assuming we had the same father. Gramma perpetrated the myth that one man sired us both. I imagine there was only so much bad behavior she could accept from her daughter. Whatever, she said Pa was a bad man. It was another reason Gramma got us out of there. If you wonder about Pa, so did I. I was told he was born in Chihuahua, Mexico and came to the U.S. to find work. What he found was my mother. He appeared now and then throughout my childhood years, always loving to Jacquie and ambivalent to me. I can say the same of him all these years later.

I don't remember the trip to Utah, but Jacquie does. She says I stayed on my tummy in the back seat, scribbling on the Big Chief tablet that Gramma got me for the trip. I vaguely recall the touch of upholstery, fuzzy as felt, beneath me. Gramma finally put a towel under me to keep the car seat from irritating my skin.

Jacquie sat up front, claiming the privilege of her superior station in life. She asked lots of questions about Mama and Papa until Gramma told her to shut her tater trap. At least that's what she told me some years later when I was old enough to listen, and Gramma was long gone, and nobody could shut Jacquie's tater trap for long.

The place Gramma lived in 1940 was Manti, south of Provo, Utah. I only remember three buildings as we left Highway 89: a mammoth glacier-white Mormon Temple, the motel cabin where we lived, and an outhouse. The rest was irrigated lawn so brilliantly green it looked artificial after our travel through desert. It was the first thing I noticed about Mormon towns that was too good to be true.

I soon forgot my mother the whore. A tiny cabin at the motel was my new reality. The Depression era might have officially ended in 1933, but it wasn't over for us. Each day was a struggle to keep our bellies semi-full.

There was a man I didn't know at the cabin, but Jacquie told me to call him Grampa. All four of us lived in that one room. Jacquie and I each had our own beds, but the cabin had no running water, no bathroom, no foundation. Gramma fixed meals on the wood stove, meals for us and meals to sell to people in other cabins. She was the kind of cook who could coax a lot out of a little; it was their only source of income.

Grampa gave me orders and jobs to do, like pumping water into buckets that he then carried inside. Thrusting that handle up and down, over my head to below my knees, was difficult, but I was obstinate and Grampa patiently let me do it. When it came to firewood we reversed roles; he chopped, and I carried the bounty inside. I don't remember much about him as I am now eighty and he has been specks of dust for many, many years. I merely recall a warmth about the word Grampa. And a smell of mown lawns, sweat, and Oxydol laundry soap wrapped around me like a blanket.

Jacquie was old enough to be sent to school. Actually, she was desperate to escape that cabin for a few hours each day. A kid named Carl and I hung around outside, a street gang of four-year-olds in the years when it was assumed if we lived through the day, we'd show up for dinner. I'm sure desert lizards still have myths they tell their neonate babies about the time the bad asses came to town to torture their kind (think the theme song from *The Good, the Bad and the Ugly*).

One day, we two banditos broke into an empty house, but were too short to get back out the window. A passerby rescued us when he heard us crying. I went home to a lecture from Gramma. Carl suffered a couple wallops from an ocotillo switch applied by his mother. Our safest afternoon activity was to hang by our knees on playground equipment until Jacquie got out of school. I never fell on my head although she accused me of it. Carl and I followed her like puppies for the rest of the day.

Gramma took us to the Mormon Sunday School every week to learn the gospels of Jesus. She left us there while she went on to her weekly Sunday School for adults. Jacquie and I were both too young for baptism; according to Mormonism, Satan can't tempt little kids because they are born innocent and without sin. But at age eight, children are fair game for the Devil, so we had that to look forward to. I didn't know what Baptism was but I wondered what evils I'd be doing as an eight-year-old that Carl and I couldn't think up at four.

I found it scary at first, that hour without Gramma. But I soon experienced the fun of crafts and activities with other kids, and I liked the Bible stories. The church staged events for us, such as egg rolls at Easter. I have a vague memory of a show with can-can girls which is, of course, highly unlikely. The open acceptance of us kids by the Latter-day Saints was unlike anything I'd ever known. I felt wanted, appreciated.

However, what struck me most about our two years in Manti wasn't the majesty of the temple or the oneness with God. The outhouse behind the cabin had that honor. Smelly, dirty, dark. Night or day, it was a house of horror, filled with ghosts and ghouls. Inside that Closet of Doom lived things with more eyes and legs than I have. Slithery things. If you sat on that board with your pants down, rats would bite at your dangly bits. Carl told me a scary story about alligators in sewers. I had no idea what an alligator was, but I'm suspicious of them to this day.

I took to peeing anywhere but there as long as I could get away with it. I wet my pants when all else failed, when good boys had given up such conduct long ago (or so I was told). I suppose I went to the desert to poop. Someone would have surely whined about human turds lying around the yard.

In 1942, Mama came to get us back from Gramma. I didn't know who she was. I cried as this stranger loaded us onto a bus and headed to California. I remember lots of men on the bus shoving each other aside to clear a seat for us. I suppose now that they were cannon fodder on the way to basic training for WWII. They were friendly. While we waited for a bus to LA in the Carson City bus depot, Mama even disappeared with a couple of them for a while, leaving Jacquie and me on a bench scarred with cigarette burns and coffee stains (today, the thought makes me shudder). While we waited, one of the men showed us how to carve the skin off an apple in one long piece. Removing skin in one piece ... sounds like heavy-handed foreshadowing for bad times ahead, doesn't it?

* * *

We moved from the little cabin in Manti to a big green house near Venice Beach, California. I thought Mama must be rich. The house was full of beautiful ladies and other kids like me. I loved it. We were allowed to go out and play during the day, but in the evenings, the kids had to stay together on the top floor. The beautiful ladies worked on the floors below us all night long, and we were told to keep our noise to a minimum.

One person looked after us. She was older than the others, the first Black woman I ever met. I asked Jacquie if she was an Indian. Jacquie, now eight, was old enough to roll her eyes. "No, silly. You're white. Indians are red. Wetbacks are brown. Coloreds are black. Milly is colored. She takes care of us when Mama is busy with her gentlemen." That was the sum total of my pre-school education in race relations.

Milly was missing some teeth and had one wandering eye. I was fascinated. That eye appeared to follow me wherever I went. One of the other kids said she had eyes in the back of her head, too. I still think it's true. There were at most eight of us, and Millie got us up and fed, sent the older kids like Jacquie off to school, and supervised the rest of us during the day. She never spanked us or slapped us. Maybe it was against the rules of the house to touch a whore's kid. I don't know.

I loved it at the big green house. When it rained we stayed inside, and a flock of beautiful ladies sometimes came up to visit us. They'd appear, dressed in colorful frills like butterflies, and hug us as clouds of perfume swirled around. They tickled us until the room vibrated with giggles. Mama was rarely with them.

On sunny days, Milly ran us down the backstairs and out onto Santa Monica Boulevard. She made us hold hands, and we slithered like a serpent between other pedestrians, down to the beach a block away. The neighborhood was a ghetto then, but I didn't know we were poor. It was such a happy place ... friends to play with, water to splash, castles to build, and Milly to keep us safe. She even provided whatever little bit of lunch she could scrape together for us. At the end of the day, she made sure we each washed away salt and sand at the outdoor shower behind the big green house. Then we tiptoed up the backstairs; the quietest one got a cookie. While I was never the cookie recipient, I remember this as the happiest time in my childhood.

It didn't last, and I was convinced after the fact, in my four-year-old wisdom, that it was all my fault. I was curious where those beautiful ladies went at night. I could hear the music from below, and it sounded like fun. So one night, after Milly read us a bedtime story, turned down the lights, and fell asleep in her chair, I snuck out. I quietly went down the stairs to the first floor where the big green house had the fanciest living room I'd ever seen. Music played on an RCA Victrola. Some people danced. Others seemed to be wrestling on the furniture. Ladies were kissing men but it looked different from the good-night kisses they gave to us kids. And their clothes seemed to be falling off.

I saw Mama on a chair. She was sitting on a man. His hand was up under her skirt where Jacquie had told me boys were never to look. That night I got a good look. At least until I said, "Mama?" and she tried to leap up. The man laughed but held onto her. "That came outta here, did it, Verna?" he said, and she yelped in pain. I ran back up the stairs and hid in my bed.

We moved away from the big green house a few days later. It must have been my fault for going downstairs. As my mother was hasty to point out, I was often a bad boy.

2.

The Shack on Venice Beach

The little house was about the size of a boot box. At $25 a month rent, it was the best Mama could afford. An electrical wire hung in the living room with a light bulb. It was the only light. The kitchen had an icebox instead of a refrigerator, and the gas stove was our only source of heat. Between the wall studs there was no insulation, just the back of the outdoor boards. The dirt floors had been covered with carpet which smelled of dankness and age. It was a real letdown after the big green house and the gentle care of Milly.

On our first day there, my sister Jacquie found me crying on the stoop behind the house. I told her I was sorry for making us move from the big green house.

"What do you mean?" she asked as I blubbered.

I told her about my night maraud to the lower levels.

"Don't be a dummy," she said, cuddling me to her narrow chest. "Mama's pregnant. That's why they kicked us out."

An older child might wonder why Mama could not figure out how to avoid babies, but I was not an older child. I was a delighted one. Our move wasn't my fault! Besides, with a baby on hand, I wouldn't be the youngest. I'd have someone to boss around.

So the big green house was gone from my life, but I found this rattletrap shack pretty appealing, too. Mama and Jacquie shared a bed in the only bedroom leaving me an enclosed sunroom tacked on to the side like a lean-to. It might have been a broken-down dump, but I had my own room!

Mama brought her business home with her. When she turned tricks in the house at night, Jacquie moved to the sofa to sleep. During the day, Jacquie and I were sent out to sit on our stoop. If Mama was playing a double-header, she sent us to the movies. If it was an away game, the two of us played the radio which we plugged into a socket next to the dangling light bulb. Or we went to the library to hear a lady read books to us.

My friend Clarence and I waited weekly for the iceman to deliver from his horse-drawn wagon. We picked up shards that fell off the blocks and sucked them like Popsicles, a great treat on a hot day. I had no idea how close to homeless we were.

I lived in the shack on Venice Beach for twelve years. Problems came and went but one constant that raised its ugly head was hunger. We didn't always eat unless our neighbors pitched in. Clarence was Black, as was most of the neighborhood. If anyone wondered why a white woman and her kids were there, they never asked me. I realize now that we were far more accepted than if it had been the other way around. Clarence's brother worked at a market on Lincoln Boulevard. He was allowed to bring home products that were too old to sell. Clarence shared this bounty with us.

Gramma had taught Jacquie a few things about cooking when we were in Utah. If Clarence scored some overripe tomatoes, Jacquie would cut them up, remove the rotten parts, and boil the rest along with stale bread. To children hungry as coyote pups, it tasted like heaven.

When I turned five, I started school. Jacquie taught me to count to one hundred and made me recite the alphabet in the mornings when she walked me to school. Much to my surprise, I got free lunches. I think the lunch lady knew I was ravenous because I believe she gave me a little extra. I ate almost anything the cafeteria pumped out. But even starving, I had the same obstinate streak that kept me out of that outhouse back in Utah. I could not abide the school's macaroni and cheese which was as dry as cardboard. But I didn't want to disappoint the lunch lady lest she go back to smaller portions. So I smeared it around on a brick ledge near the base of the table where I sat. I wondered for the rest of my grade school years if it hardened there forever, the same consistency as the grout.

* * *

Gramma lived with us for a while after Grampa died, hell bent on saving our souls at the Mormon Church. She enrolled Jacquie and me in Sunday School once again. Jacquie was now old enough to be baptized. I was still too young to understand Mormonism, but I continued to enjoy the stories and time with other kids. Gramma also took us to the free community sings on the beach in Ocean Park. I loved them; I was the only little boy in Venice Beach who knew all the words to *I've Got a Lovely Bunch of Coconuts*. I can still belt out a handful of standards that were old before I was born, a talent that I'm rarely asked to display.

Gramma meant to help our home life, but mostly she hindered it. I loved her, but she and Mama tangled like alley cats. I picked up words that could make a sailor blush. My teacher took me aside often, trying to redeem my vocabulary. Finally in frustration she asked, "Where do you learn words like that, Wayne?"

"From Mama when she talks to Gramma. What's wrong with it?"

In addition to an obstinate nature and a mouth in need of soap, I was held back a year for screwing up spelling and reading tests. Nobody knew what dyslexia was back then. I just got a reputation as a sluggish learner, a reputation that followed me well into junior high. Stubborn. A potty-mouth. Lazy. Not the best qualifications for success. But I had one talent nobody could deny: I could draw like an angel. Lovely landscapes, portraits, fancy cars. While the other kids were applying engorged heads to stick figure bodies, I was creating scenes of the beach and sweeping hills to the north. My ark with animals was a recognizable boat filled with recognizable species, plus a unicorn or two. I drew at home in pencil or crayon or chalk on any paper I could find. Gramma gave me a little tin of watercolors.

My teacher said to me, "Wayne. You can't read all that well, and I'm nearly afraid to hear half of what comes out of your mouth. But with talent like that, you can be an artist one day." She then chuckled. "You should go to the Sorbonne in Paris to study. Maybe the French can handle your dirty words."

She no doubt forgot what she'd said by the next day. I remembered it the rest of my life. That's what the right teacher at the right time can do for a child with no father and a questionable mother.

* * *

My mother held down the occasional job, but in general she was a 'soiled dove' whose clientele was not exactly top-of-the-line. She was always poor, always tired, and in the early months in Venice, pregnant. She must have been miserable, and she willfully spread her misery around to us. I heard and saw things that other five-year-olds can't imagine.

One Saturday, Mama had an all-day-stand. She applied her makeup, best dress, and high heels, then dropped Jacquie and me at the Criterion Theater in Santa Monica. It was a double feature: one was *Lassie Come Home* and the other a Mickey Rooney comedy called *Girl Crazy*. The best part was the cartoons that showed at the end. Jacquie left me to watch them and went out to see if Mama was there to pick us up at the appointed time. She wasn't. So Jacquie came back in to join me. Mama was rarely where she said she'd be on time. But it wasn't long before an usher came to get us. "Your ma's out front and yikes, is she out for blood."

We hustled out, and sure enough, Mama was in the car and yelling at us "little shits" as we scrambled out of the lobby, under the marquee, and tumbled into the car, Jacquie in the front and me in the back. She continued to shout as she sped across the first canal bridge. Maybe her date had been a really bad one. Whatever, she lost control of the vehicle. The parked car we plunged into was just off the second bridge.

I was thrown up to the ceiling of the car, banged my head, and everything went dark. When I came to, my body was crammed onto the floor in the back seat. I was so woozy I could hardly sit upright but I struggled to the seat. I saw flashing lights, heard sirens, and saw Jacquie on the hood of the car. She'd gone through the windshield (this was in the years before safety glass might have stopped her).

Somebody covered Jacquie's face with a towel, and big men in uniforms got all three of us into an ambulance that rushed away. They didn't let me near Jacquie's gurney, although I tried to scramble back there. A man in the front held onto me. Then I was left on a bench in the Santa Monica Hospital, in front of the nurses' station, while Mama and Jacquie were rolled away.

This was terror like I'd never felt before. I was five and all alone.

Mama and Jacquie! Are they dead?

As I cried in confusion, a man came and sat next to me. He waited for me to look up at him. Then he put an arm around me, stayed with me a while, and said everything would be okay. It helped. A nurse told me later he was Edgar Bergen. I've had a soft spot for Charlie McCarthy and Mortimer Snerd ever since.

Mama lost her baby in that accident. And my sister came home with her entire head wrapped in bandages. It was a horror show. I was terrified Jacquie would look like Boris Karloff in *The Mummy* when those bandages were removed.

And, in fact, she did have deep scars on her beautiful face, scars that lasted a lifetime. As she grew, she got very good at hiding the worst ones with make-up. I have to believe those scars deeply marked her soul as well as her face, but Jacquie didn't complain about her loss, at least not to her little brother. She continued to find comfort for her anguish in the Mormon religion.

* * *

I began to see the world for what it was. First, everybody had to work. And that meant me, too. I could no longer think that life was mostly for the fun of it.

When Gramma lived with us, she was big on assigning chores, singlehandedly destroying my free Saturday afternoons. She decreed that she and I would make laundry day easier on my mother.

Mama did all our clothes down on her knees, washing everything in our bathtub, rinsing, then drying on a line strung between the house and a palm. Everything dried gritty from beach sand in the air. Gramma took over the job and roped me in, too. I loaded all the dirty clothes in a wire cart with mismatched wheels, and we squeaked our way down the street to the Help Yourself Laundry. The place was hot, steamy, and had damp slippery tiles. If you dropped something on the floor, it might give you malaria, according to

Gramma whose grim description of the disease taught me to be extremely careful.

The machines all looked ferocious. We jammed our clothes in two washers along with Fels-Naptha, and stood back. When the machines were done churning and sloshing, we squeezed the wet duds through their wringers. Everything was dunked in cold water then wrung again. I never failed getting drenched in the process.

Next came the tumble dryers that got hot enough to kill ticks and dust mites, but left clothes stiffer and smaller than they were when we brought them in. We folded everything, then wheeled the clean load back to the shack in Gramma's cart. Gone were my Saturday afternoons with Clarence. It was an outrage. Surely Mama's knees weren't worth such a sacrifice on my behalf.

Mama eventually kicked Gramma out. I had no idea why they fought so vigorously, taking deadly aim at each other's deepest wounds. I loved Gramma and wanted her to stay, but even I knew it couldn't be. But there was an upside: I figured Mama would go back to washing clothes down on her knees. Instead, she made Jacquie and me continue the trips to the Help Yourself Laundry. It gave her a way to get us out of the house. Saturdays were still shot.

3.

Dirty Ernie

Jacquie and I loved movies. Mama sometimes gave us enough money to take a bus to whatever theater was showing one we wanted to see. That was just about any movie. Movies taught me about romance. And I do mean romance. The son of a shady lady learns about sex early on. Movies didn't feature that. They taught me about long relationships, chocolate and flowers, lingering kisses, loving glances. That's what I saw on the silver screen, not merely the sordid relationships grinding away in the bedroom at home. I bought into the fantasy. I wanted the happily-ever-after. The goal followed me into my adult years. If it happened in the movies, it must happen in real life, too.

While I was ready for romance at a very young age, there was a problem. I had no physical interest in girls. Not ever. I was far more interested in my own anatomy than theirs. It took

19

me until junior high to figure out what was wrong, and when I did, it felt like a disaster. I was different from anybody I knew, maybe anybody else in the whole world. No wonder Mama didn't love me.

I had nowhere to turn with my questions. Little boys in the 1940s and 50s had a dearth of information. Imagine if anybody had explained that my feelings were natural, nothing to be ashamed of, an acceptable part of me. Years of inner turmoil and self-loathing lay ahead due to those few missing pearls of wisdom.

I always clung to Jacquie for direction and guidance on anything, but she wouldn't have known any more than I did about boys preferring boys. I did ask her to teach me how to kiss. The lesson was a miserable failure, but provided great giggles then and for years after. She might have known her brother wasn't like other boys, but she wouldn't have known why. It was a boyfriend of hers who unknowingly gave me a hint. He was helping her paint a wall, and Jacquie asked me to pull a paint receipt from his back pocket. His pants were tight, and I had to rummage around. I was feeling a boy's anatomy for the very first time.

Holy kamoley!

I didn't know the word for it, but I was homosexual. The word gay was still in the future.

I was popular in junior high and had a group of friends for football scrimmages or horse on the basketball court at the beach. I was growing tall and muscular; athletics came easily. One day, sweaty from play, we were taking a break. A friend pulled a photo from his wallet. It was creased with age and excessive handling. He passed it around. It was a risqué photo of a naked man and woman. The other boys checked out the woman with great attention. I checked out the man. Who knew there were pictures like this? I didn't get that photo out of my brain for months. So. I preferred boys, and it was a secret. My mother was a prostitute, and it was a secret. I never invited friends home to see our poverty, because it was a secret. My reality was shameful. I learned to hide everything about myself behind a façade. People found me friendly, bright, even elected me to student offices. But nobody knew me.

* * *

I had decided to go to the Sorbonne in Paris. I had no real idea what the Sorbonne was, or where Paris was for that matter, when that grade school teacher instilled in me the goal. But I'd looked it up. I was well-known at the library since I'd been a customer starting with the Children's Read-Aloud Hour when I was a preschooler. I fantasized the teacher had recognized a greatness within me completely unnoticed by my family or anyone else. They were thinking coloring books while I was envisioning the Tate, El Prado, MoMa, the Louvre. People would be in awe and think I was a brooding genius as I painted my way through life. I would be a jillionaire. Boy, wouldn't Mama be proud of me then.

From the ages of twelve to sixteen, I was a diligent paperboy, delivering the *Examiner* in the morning before school, and the *Evening Outlook* after school, saving nearly all my money. My Gramma helped me open a bank account that my mother couldn't pilfer. I had a goal, and the grit to get there. If Paris meant rising in the wee hours every single day, I could do it. I went to work so early in that questionable neighborhood, I was often the only soul visible on empty streets. Bandits might mug me, or werewolves might eat me, or Indians shoot arrows through my heart. Hey, I was twelve, and imagination was never in short supply.

The first day I started the route, two cops stopped me. I explained what I was doing on a bike before dawn. After that, when they passed in their patrol car, they would blink their lights at me. I felt safe knowing they were there.

Another man kept an eye out for me, too. I stopped each morning at a little shop for coffee and pastry. Giuseppe, the owner, watched for me through the shop's big front window, and he'd pour me a cup so it was ready when I arrived. One morning, I saw police lights around the shop. It had been burgled, and Giuseppe was shot. He survived but never opened for business again. Since I was not family, the hospital didn't allow me in to see him.

It seemed that every time I got close to someone, something bad happened to them. I determined that was the way of the world, precarious and dangerous. A good person had to watch out for the people around him, whether they deserved it or not. A sense of obligation awakened in me, one that weaves through the upcoming pages of my story.

I was the first to arrive at the newspaper office in the mornings. In addition to being obstinate, I was organized. Or maybe just fussy since I've always wanted things tidy. My first chore was to haul bundles of newspapers in from the curb where delivery trucks dropped them. I counted out the right number for each carrier, folded the papers, tied them, and set them up for the routes. The other kids loved it, and so did my manager. He gave me a couple extra bucks a day to come back to the office after my route, and answer complaint calls about the kids' deliveries. I still managed to ride my bike at a furious pace to get to grade school on time.

One customer, whom I thought of as a crusty old fart, complained about me and canceled the paper. My manager went to several people on my route who each claimed I was doing a fine job. He didn't fire me. He praised me! I needed affection as badly as a rescue dog, because I sure didn't get it at home. My boss believed in me more wholeheartedly than my own mother. I took pride in doing well; it made me strive to be a better student and employee throughout the rest of my life.

* * *

Some of my mother's men were nice to Jacquie and me, and some ignored us. We became used to having them around. When I was in the early stages of recognizing I was gay, I also became aware that all these men weren't such good "friends" as my mother referred to them. Mama often had bruises, a sore arm, or a reddened cheek.

Yet, at no time did she ever accept a hug or sympathy from me. Maybe she did from Jacquie, at night when no man was there, and mother and daughter shared the bed. Jacquie says she never did. That makes me very sad as I write it. At some point, I must have understood that Jacquie and I were no more than mistakes in Mama's life, mistakes she lived with out of duty rather than love.

I suppose that's why Jacquie and I were so protective of each other. One night Mama met a man in a bar and brought him home. Both were drunk enough to wake me up with their pawing and grunting. From the sunroom I could see the man was sloppy, grabbing at her ass as she kicked off her shoes. But the real problem was for Jacquie, who was asleep in the bed.

That night, my sister didn't have time to vacate for the sofa before Mama and the man crowded into bed on top of her. She was pinned down. The man groped Jacquie through her nightie. Maybe he thought he had a handful of my mother. Whatever, Jacquie shrieked. I ran into the room and pulled him off her long enough for her to scamper out. He was much bigger than me, could have leveled me, but lost interest after cuffing me away. He turned his attention back to my mother. Jacquie climbed into bed with me in the sunroom, and we huddled through the night until he left the next morning.

We both knew it was only a matter of time before some disaster happened. It spooked Jacquie. She married a boy when she was only seventeen so she could move out of that nightmare shack. She promised me she'd always be just a phone call away. But I was now alone with my mother.

* * *

I called him Dirty Ernie, although an adult would have come up with something far more grotesque. He was a long-term client of Mama's, still coming around when I was sixteen. To this day, I cannot understand why she let him. He was a brute, a danger.

Mama had a part-time job doing the books at the Aragon Ballroom. When she came home carrying a bottle of whiskey in a brown paper bag, I knew Dirty Ernie was on his way. The first thing he would do is turn the radio up as loud as it would go. Then they disappeared into the bedroom. The music was to cover the noise they made. He was intent on hurting her, and she let him. I could do nothing but leave the house and seek out a movie where life was blissful. Mama would make Ernie his dinner, then they would go back into the bedroom for round two.

When I got home one evening, the two of them were still at it. I quietly went to my own cubby in the sunroom. Early in the morning, I heard Mama rise, make coffee, and leave for her day job. I assumed I was alone, so I rolled over and went back to sleep.

I didn't hear Dirty Ernie come into my room. I awoke as he pulled the covers away. He was naked. I was confused and frightened, with no idea what he was doing, but I yelled at him to get out. He hit me across the face, a strong man's blow meant to disable a boy. He grappled at my Jockey shorts, ripping them off as I tried to get up. Then he pinned me to the bed and penetrated my anus. I shrieked and bucked but could not dislodge him.

When it was over, I was in pain but even more appalled. What had just happened? He warned me not to tell anybody, or he'd hurt me more the next time. After he left, I stayed still with shock, bleeding anally. I finally limped to the bathroom, ran a tub of water, and soaked until the water and I were both cold.

I didn't tell anyone. But I made a plan.

Dirty Ernie came back the next weekend. I waited quietly in the living room, knowing he'd come out of my mother's bedroom to go to the bathroom sometime during the night. When he did, I lunged, taking a full swing with a baseball bat. He fell like a rag doll, roaring in pain. I kicked him as hard as I could in the balls, then sank on top of him to smash him in the face. I released all the rage I'd ever felt onto that monster of a man. But Mama was pulling my hair and slapping me, trying to get me off him. Without physically hurting her, I had to back off. By then, neighbors were pounding on the door, yelling the cops were on the way.

I backed away from Ernie who was comatose on the floor. Choking back tears, I rode my bike to my best friend Pete's home, away from my ghetto to a much better neighborhood. Pete's dad taught at a city college, and they lived in what to me was a mansion. That night, I told his father some of what had happened, enough for him to say I could stay with them until I had someplace to go.

Dirty Ernie never pressed charges. And I never went back. It would be many years before I saw my mother again. Any home had to be better than hers.

* * *

Sixteen and homeless. I would never have been able to rent a place if I hadn't had money for Paris stashed away. I took some of that money now, to rent a one-room apartment on the boardwalk at Venice Beach, not far from Muscle Beach. I had a hot plate, a narrow iron-framed bed, and a bathroom sink. The actual bathroom was out the door and to the left. Shades of that Utah outhouse came back to haunt me, but at sixteen I was far more of a match for spiders and ghosts. Hell, I'd beaten the snot out of Dirty Ernie so I was quite the hombre.

I tried to project that image of a tough guy. But oh, how the specter of that rape violated my dreams and sickened my heart. I hadn't even known that boys could be raped. I quickly recovered physically, but mentally I've carried it for life. I was scared and lonely, in need of comfort, world weary as I left my childhood behind.

4.

First Love

It was just a few days past my sixteenth birthday. I'd left home for good, it was 1953, and I still had a dream of Paris. That dream didn't have to make sense, it didn't have to sound rational, but it had to stay mine. It was all I owned. If it survived, I would, too.

The paper routes morning and afternoon were all well and good, but who ever heard of a rich paperboy? What money I could make went first for rent and food, a tiny bit for movies, and the lion's share to my savings.

A neighbor said he could get me a job at the Venice post office sorting mail, but I'd have to lie about my age. You had to be eighteen to sort mail which struck me as weird, since even a dyslexic like me conquered the alphabet in grade school. This was the first time I questioned government regulations, beginning a long life of such doubts.

I needed false identification. An art project! My very first one for money. I would falsify my birth certificate. If I couldn't make it as an artist maybe art forger would do (except the forger usually gets shot in the movies). Jacquie came to my rescue as she so often had. She loaned me her birth certificate. With a borrowed Kodak Brownie box camera, I photographed it and mine. From the prints, I cut the date off hers then pasted it over mine. Another photo and Voila! I was nineteen and could prove it. And it worked. Or it was so bad, the postmaster instantly knew it was a phony and found the scam funny. She could hardly have believed the gawky towhead in front of her, just growing into the size of his own feet and developing a fluff of a mustache, was really nineteen. Whatever, the job was mine.

I said goodbye to the newspaper business and went to the post office after school and football practice. My shift had four sorters, and we didn't finish until deep into the night, depending on the amount of mail. We developed a kind of dance routine around each other. One bopped to the California mail bags, two of us boogie-woogied around bags for all other states, and another strolled through foreign deliveries. We could have staged our own chorus line. I loved this job.

In the night, I biked home to my apartment on the beach to shower and sleep. The next day, I did it again, always tired and often hungry. But money was flowing in. I dropped out of football because I couldn't travel with the high school team. Instead, I concentrated on French and art classes in school. I worked at the post office until I actually *was* nineteen.

Under pressure from the guys at school who thought I was too shy to date, I went to my senior prom. Yes, with a girl. I liked her because she knew a bunch about sports, and she was an athlete back in the day when girls were taught that sweating in public would destroy their social lives forever. I knew what boys were supposed to do on prom night, and it became my first sexual experience with a female. We explored each other, and I realized I wasn't all that sure how to insert Tab A into Slot B. We had a nice time touching as we were both curious, but she didn't have the right equipment to play the game the way I liked it.

Many years later, at a class reunion, she told me she was gay. I was her first experience with a boy, and she had found my equipment lacking as well. I remember her to this day, if not with great passion, then at least with great affection. Wherever you are, Grace, I hope your partner is a helluva hottie.

* * *

I was still sixteen when love came calling. It was an honest-to-goodness romance of the type I only saw at the movies. I wanted the full *From Here to Eternity* experience, replacing Deborah

Kerr in the arms of Burt Lancaster. But I was fairly sure Burt wasn't likely to come my way.

I could imagine it, though, one night as I walked home from the Dome Theater on the boardwalk in Ocean Park. I smelled the ocean in the breeze, saw the footprints in the sand of all the people who gathered there that day. I was feeling seriously lonely, hopeless, and drenched with self-pity.

And there my romance was. He appeared ahead of me, looming out of the darkness. White tee-shirt, blue jeans, dark hair, and a killer smile. I tried to be discreet as I gawked, but what sixteen-year-old boy is discreet? My eyes must have been like cartoon eyes that bug out at the sight of a marvelous dessert. I remember the sound of the surf and the symphony of passionate strings that filled my head.

Did I pick him up, or did he pick me up? He was much older, maybe thirty and on the hunt for a young man like me. Or maybe I was on the hunt for an experienced man like him. What does it matter now?

We stopped, smiled, and walked on together. He matched my pace and direction. In time, we sat on a park bench to talk. He told me he worked nights at Douglas Aircraft. I told him about the post office and about Paris. I neglected to mention my age; since I was masquerading as a nineteen-year-old at work, I hoped I came across as one here on the boardwalk, as well.

We sat for a long time, not touching but chatting like parrots with each other. It was exciting but scary, too. The term 'gay' wasn't even invented back then ... we were a couple of filthy homosexuals. Just being such a vile person was illegal, much less acting like one. As people walked by, I stopped talking for fear we would be overheard, although nothing dirty was said. In the process, I probably *did* make us look guilty.

His name was James. He invited me to join him for breakfast the next day, which was a Sunday. He said to bring along a bathing suit. I desperately wanted to go, but I couldn't afford such a luxury as a meal out. He must have seen that pain as I dithered; at least he clarified that it was on him.

I was so afraid of doing something wrong. I'd rarely been to a restaurant and then only a diner. I knew next to nothing about how to order, what to eat. Only once had I seen anything like a fancy table. Gramma had taken Jacquie and me to a Thanksgiving meal at one of her brother's. It was the first time I'd ever had butter. Along with all the other fixings, they even had three pies. These were riches I'd never known before.

So to go out for a meal? With James? The ache of that anticipation hurts me still. What if I spilled anything, or used the wrong utensil, or said a stupid thing? He'd know I was nothing more than a poor boy, trying to lift myself out of the slum.

I was terrified. But I went. I convinced myself he would never show up. But there he was, waiting for me at a cafe on the boardwalk at Rose Ave. He was even more gorgeous than I remembered.

There must be a movie crew filming this!

The hostess sat us outside, under a colorful umbrella to moderate the sun. James said he'd been here before, and asked if he could do the ordering for me (only as I aged did I realize how kind he was). He ordered cafe au lait and fresh-fruit crêpes, in honor of Paris. I was thrilled he remembered what I'd talked about the night we met, but I'd never heard of such food as this. It tasted like heaven to me. At the end of our meal, as we left the cafe, he reached over and brushed a bit of powdered sugar from my mouth. Then he licked that sweetness from his fingers.

Any resistance I might have had was swept away in that single gesture.

He took me for a drive north along the coast on Highway 101. The powerful Oldsmobile purred. It smelled new and clean and sounded as happy as I felt. It was about an hour before James pulled into a motel. He went in the office to rent a room so we could change to our swimsuits and take a plunge into the motel's huge pool.

Some of you are screaming "BE CAREFUL ... DON'T GO IN THERE!" Again, I remind you this was sixty-some years ago. Back then, we weren't so likely to stick screwdrivers in each other's eyes or eat each other's livers along with fava beans. I was young but totally willing, desperate to explore how sex might differ from rape. I not only went in that room, I grabbed him.

My first kiss with a man was not at all like kissing my sister. Neither of us giggled. It sent blood rushing to my head and all the other right locations. We were gentle and eager as the bed cushioned us. I hoped it would never end, and I was absolutely convinced that James was mine, and I was his. Cue the violins!

I will now close the door on this scene, but you can open it in your imaginations. James and I did finally make it to the pool. I discovered then that all the couples were males. I was flabbergasted that such places existed where we could be ourselves. It felt like sanctuary, but it was still illegal, what we were doing. Officers of the law, with nothing better to do, could bust down the doors at any time. I was certain I would be rushed off to jail. But if it meant time with James, it was very worth it.

We became steady weekend companions. During the week, I continued going to high school, working at the post office, and living in my room. But I moved to James's home each Saturday morning and stayed through Sunday. We adopted a rescue dog together. He bought me new clothes. His friends became my friends. I felt liberated, able to live honestly. This was a joyous time for me. James even finally accepted the fact that I was sixteen, although he was pretty pissed when I admitted that little nugget.

We did have one stumbling block, though, and it was a big one. Paris.

* * *

I lived with James for four years, moving in full-time after high school graduation. We were happy as any new couple, although our relationship did skew in a teacher/student direction. James, substantially older than I was, had money, a career, a community. I knew so little outside the hellhole which was the Venice of my youth. He taught me everything about socializing, etiquette, world view. James built up my confidence, made me feel that there was something worth knowing about me. I loved him as a lover, true, but also as a mentor. My attitude that most things will work out is largely attributable to this very lucky first romance, the likes of which I didn't find again for decades.

We did the normal couple things, each with our own duties: I mowed the lawn, walked the dog, cleaned the house. As the chef, he was amazed how much I could wolf down. James was a movie buff, just like me so on nights that he wasn't at Douglas, and I wasn't at the post office, we often made a movie/dinner date. Or he would sneak me into a club where he was scheduled to drum with a band.

When I graduated, it was clear that I still didn't have the money to head to France. I figured I'd need $80 a month, and I was short. James helped me get a job at Douglas in the parts department. It paid a lot more than the post office, and we could commute together.

Every strand of our lives braided together. Romance, work, entertainment, we shared it all. And my leaving for Paris threatened every bit of it. If we split, it would cause a total start-over for each of us.

At first James supported art school wholeheartedly. He'd even offered to pay for the trip! He probably thought it was good for a kid to have a goal. I doubt he believed it would ever really happen. But the day came that I was accepted by the Sorbonne and passed the written French test they sent me to complete. I could start classes in March 1956.

James tried, but could not truly grasp how this was the mainspring of my life, how that dream had carried me through days of being beaten with a hairbrush by my mother, of hunger, of rape, of never having anything if I didn't work for it myself. I could not walk away from studying art in Paris now. The dream had become more important than the reality, so it hovered on the horizon like a dark cloud.

Our last year together was bittersweet. We knew the fantasy life we lived was coming to an end. James suggested I study art in LA or we go to France as a vacation, but of course, that was not the same thing. I would be gone at least two years. The best we could hope was that James would visit on his holidays. And he said he would write to me every week.

I left Los Angeles Union Station by train to New York in early February 1956. James drove me to the station and stood on the platform as I boarded. Tears streamed down my face as we left the station. My last view of James was of him waving, tears on his own face. You've seen that goodbye scene in the movies a million times.

The difference this time? I never saw my lover again, and that's not how romances are supposed to end.

5.

Paris!

The Super Chief was known as the *Train of the Stars* in the 1950s on its run from LA to NY with a layover in Chicago. It was one of the fastest trains in the world. Passengers were practically guaranteed by railroad hucksters they'd meet the likes of Paul Newman, Gloria Swanson, Janet Leigh, Jimmy Durante, and partake in sparkling conversations in the Pleasure Dome Lounge.

James had bought me a suit, because nobody traveled in tee-shirts and jeans in those days. Nonetheless, a low-end passenger such as me would never see the lounges or sleeping cars, much less who occupied them. While I might have made the effort to scout them out on any other occasion, I was grieving over James. I sat in my second-class seat and barely moved until we reached the Chicago Dearborn Station.

We had a twelve-hour layover. I staggered off into cold so brutal I'd never felt the like. I located the YMCA and finally slept, exhausted from over-spilled emotion. In the morning, I boarded again in time to head for New York. What little I remember of Chicago has been wiped away by that icy wind they call the Hawk.

Maybe the freezing temperature knocked the edge off my grief. Or more likely, I'd dealt with so much grief by then that I knew how to compartmentalize it. When the train pulled into New York, I was feeling more than a little excitement.

New York! What a dream for a kid whose tallest building so far was the Los Angeles City Hall. The weather was mild in the city, and I gawked at New Yorkers for two days, walking the streets amidst them as they shined shoes, sold hot dogs, took subways, ran for buses, cussed like sailors. Everyone moved like they were practicing for marathons; this was definitely not the California amble. I smiled at a man hauling a block of ice, remembering the iceman in Venice; he said, "What the fuck do you want?" and I laughed aloud. I visited art galleries, picturing my work on their walls. It was only a matter of time. I knew James and I would leave California and move to this marvelous place. If that grade school teacher had mentioned the Guggenheim instead of the Sorbonne, then I'd have arrived at my destination.

But it had been the Sorbonne. I needed to get to France. I had it all planned out. In New York, I had a job waiting on the Cunard Line's SS *United States*. I would work as a cabin boy, and my passage to France would be free. We set sail after three days of intensive training for all the incoming staff. Our room was a big sleeping area with lockers and bunk beds. Passenger rooms were a different thing altogether.

* * *

While the *United States* was the fastest ocean liner in her day, the ads touted that *Getting There Was Half the Fun*. Not necessarily so. My trip was "the worst crossing of all time," according to the old salts on the crew. The Atlantic Ocean rocked and rolled, at one time casting us like flotsam so far over that one of the propellers actually lifted out of the water. Everyone onboard was wretchedly ill except a handful of us impervious to *mal de mer*, if you'll pardon my French. At first I felt rather superior, as though I were a seasoned traveler. But then the bad news hit me: I had to clean cabins where passengers were sick for days. And let me tell you, a rich man's cabin may have a sprawling living room and astounding views, but he's as miserable as a poor man when holding tight to the toilet bowl.

All the rich food for the guests was given to anyone who could still eat. We hearty souls feasted on eggs Benedict, filet mignon, lobster, the best coffee in the world. It wasn't just a kindness; all that food would be dumped when we docked in France, making way for new stores to return to New York.

It was such a thrill for me to try out my French, but I soon began to question the abilities of Miss Peevish, the Venice High School French teacher. I was undeterred, and people were understanding. On the train from the Port of Le Havre to Paris, I realized I didn't understand a lick of *real* French. People who knew English laughed at my terrible American accent and began pointing at things out the window and pronouncing "horse" or "bicycle" in French, the way it should be said. When I arrived in Paris, one fellow train passenger took me to the subway and told me where to get off for the Sorbonne.

For the first time, I began to feel a sense of fear. A city I didn't know with a language I didn't speak, and I was to go to school? With dread, I went to the office of the Frenchman who was to be my advisor at the Sorbonne. He nodded as he listened to me introduce myself. Then he said with my lack of French pronunciation and comprehension, I would not be accepted at this school or likely, any other.

Ah! My dream was gutted and dying on that dear man's floor. Seeing I was about to panic, he took pity on a lost American boy. While the French-as-a-second-language courses were all filled in Paris, he said I could catch the class in Geneva. With it under my belt, I could come back to the Sorbonne. I signed up, he arranged lodging for me there, and on my first day in Paris, I left for Switzerland.

* * *

So. A short detour to another city. The countries seemed like miniatures to me when it had taken me days to cross the United States. On the train to Geneva, I discovered that other passengers were doing the same thing. They wanted a course in practical language skills to make them sound local. Students from many countries began quizzing each other as we rode the rails. We practiced, "What a beautiful day" and "The pen of my aunt" and similar phrases all the way, learning the French accent as well as the words. We bonded, the Swiss kids and the Germans and a Spaniard. I now had friends. We exchanged addresses and promised to get together. I longed for James to share my experiences, of course, but I no longer felt alone in the world.

When I got off the train, a student waiting for me took me to the apartment where I would stay. There were five of us, all going to L'Alliance Francaise to learn the language. Each of us had his own room, but we shared meals and a kitchen. My new friends took me to the shops, a different one for bread than for milk than for canned goods. They didn't eat meat, and I soon found out why: the only red meat I could afford would have been horse. I ate a lot of fish.

In class, we could only speak French. We began with the basics of each letter, the many ways to pronounce it, and how an accent mark changed it. We sounded out words phonetically and memorized them, as well as whether they were masculine or feminine. In the second week we began to read aloud. When called on, we had to read whole pages without errors.

The class was small and not everyone made it through. My roommates and I shared the kitchen table many times, studying in the evenings. One of them, a Canadian, taught me how to wrestle during study breaks. It had been his high school sport. I was strong and agile, bigger than he was, and I finally managed to pin him. As I rolled off, I realized I had a boner. I quickly got up and turned away to sit at the table. We never wrestled again.

I missed James. I missed sex. My roommates all went to bed earlier than I did, and I couldn't understand why. Then one night, I retired early, too. I opened my bedroom window and could hear the other guys at their windows.

What's the deal?

Across a clearing was an apartment building whose tenants left their lights on. Europeans were far less inhibited than Americans. I realized staring into those many lit windows, that couples were going at it like rabbits. Not just men and women, but men and men, women and women. I had every intention of being loyal to James, but oh my goodness, Switzerland made me ache!

I wondered if the French behaved this way. Were they so open to homosexual couples? I could see I needed to learn a little more of the language. The kind of words I'd like to whisper to James.

Geneva was rustic compared to the mega-city I'd briefly visited in France. It was growing fast in the years after the war, attracting foreign workers from many places and corporations with money. I knew nothing about history but could still feel the energy of the city. What Americans called a "can-do" spirit. The center of town was at the end of Lake Geneva where it met the Rhone. Almost nobody drove ... my first major purchase in Europe was a bike.

The few weeks I was there, I biked everywhere. I lost some of the weight that I'd carried since playing football back home. I saw the UN headquarters, the Jet d'Eau in the lake that shot water one hundred and forty meters into the air, took weekend camping trips to the mountains. Friends and I would pedal up the heights, muscles straining, then race back down. Even today, I feel the exhilaration of youth and power from those long flights downhill. The landscape and the freedom were equally breathtaking.

I passed my language test. It was time to get on with my art education so I headed back to France, at least a little wiser about living in a foreign land. This interval in Switzerland was no doubt a great buffer to digging in at a foreign school.

* * *

In California, a mission might date back to the eighteenth century. Nothing (except maybe Gramma) was older than that. But the Sorbonne's roots went back to the thirteenth century. History lived in the Latin Quarter, venerable and intellectual. I was overawed. What seemed possible from the distant Venice, CA seemed way out of my reach in Paris. And worst of all, when I signed up for a class schedule, I learned I must take more than art classes. I needed art history and French history. I could have done that. But I needed other basics as well, choices in math and sciences. I only wanted to learn to paint. The Sorbonne was not right for me, or me for it.

Depressed, I went to speak with an art professor. Professor Du Boise was a handsome man. From my age of nineteen, I guessed him to be old ... maybe in his forties, but who can say how right or wrong I was? He had a thick thatch of dark hair, a three-o'clock shadow, bushy brows, and eyes as dark as espresso. He listened carefully.

"So you are not so interested in a degree? Merely in painting?"

"I think that's the size of it."

"What if a Sorbonne instructor taught art classes as a tutor?" He raised those eyebrows like question marks.

My depression began to lift. "Is there such a person?"

"You are speaking with him now."

I was ecstatic. That night I moved into an apartment that had provided cheap housing for students since the 1930s. The next morning I applied for the government-sanctioned ID card that the concierge demanded to see.

Six of us lived together in the downtrodden building which still showed signs of destruction from WWII. It was in a very dangerous part of town, populated primarily by Arab families struggling to get by. A fringe group in their midst was intent on blowing up the Eiffel Tower and other locations. They mostly failed, but the area was given a 10 p.m. curfew. Police walked the district carrying machine guns.

The following day, my class with Professor Du Boise began. I assumed it would be watercolor, but I was wrong; we started out with oils. Once again I felt disconsolate. I had spent so much in Geneva that I could not afford the expensive oil paints; I had to stick to my meager $80 per month budget.

I explained to the professor that I couldn't take the class after all. He nodded then told me to wait while he gave his other tutored students their first class project. When they were underway, he came back to me. "Here is a tube of black paint and a tube of white." He also directed me to three brushes, a canvas, pallet, and easel. "Now paint this." He pointed to a gathering of fruit, a glass, and a bowl that was arranged on a table.

A still life in black and white? Since grade school I had drawn in pencil only. I had untutored experience with how objects reflected light and caught shadows. I began to work.

For the morning, I disappeared from that classroom and into my head where the banana, mango, and bowl replaced any other thought I might have had. The time passed, and I became aware of movement as the other students gathered their things and left the room.

Professor Du Boise came to stand behind me and view the canvas on my easel. At last he said, "About one-quarter of the people who tried this class today will not be back. I will give you the paints they leave behind." In no time at all, I was painting in color.

I was probably in love with him right then. But not as you are thinking. He was not gay ... in fact, one pretty mademoiselle seemed to require far more tutoring than the rest of us. She also appeared to get lost often because the professor needed to accompany her to her apartment.

Why on earth did the man keep putting up with me? It was a puzzle I enjoyed unscrambling. He liked my work, and he liked me. He hadn't tutored many Americans. And he loved Hollywood movies. He might have gotten the idea I actually knew some of the stars.

The class was emotional for me. I had raw talent but was as untrained as an athlete who'd never thrown a ball. I failed and then failed again. Du Boise was a benevolent despot who pushed techniques, use of color, breaking up space. He taught that you oil paint from the top of the canvas down, establishing background first. It had to dry completely before the foreground details were added. He taught us to *see* when we looked at an object. Did it cast a shadow and where was the shadow the darkest? How did light change the color from back to front? If we did it wrong, he returned our canvases and told us to look again.

Sometimes he walked us through one of his own paintings, and we tried to copy what he was doing. I was amazed how the others approached the assignment in so many ways, some brilliant and others with no control of their brushes.

He gave us each the same assignments, and the class critiqued each other, two paintings in a week's time. It took some doing, but I finally learned how to hold my temper at a critical review and actually listened to what others were telling me. In time, I became a favorite in the class.

One evening Professor Du Boise and his wife took me to dinner. They ordered wine.

I felt as though invisible reins pulled me up tight. I had not been to a Mormon church since I was a child with Gramma. I'd been too young to know doctrine, but I did know alcohol was a no-no. Mama certainly indulged and it did her no favors. I had to tell them *something*.

"I was baptized Mormon. We don't drink. I don't know why," I said, hanging my head like a shamed dog.

The professor's eyes widened. "But wine is not drinking. Wine is life!" He was, after all, very French. He poured, and I drank. The warm blush I felt after glass number two was a fine moment of open *bon ami* for me. As I rode home on the Subway that night, every Frenchman aboard was my best friend, and I whistled as I walked home.

It was after 10 p.m. when I felt the machine gun shoved between my ribs, terrifying me instantly. The police officers demanded my papers and were amazed I was American. "In this area? We thought all Americans were rich!" They walked me to my door and left. I never missed curfew again.

Our live-in concierge met me that night, worry in her dark eyes. I told her I was fine, that I had merely sampled too much good French wine. She was the tiniest adult I'd ever known, a willow just five feet tall. I believe she was always awake, keeping an eye on the students when she wasn't washing the stairs or cleaning the toilets on the landings between floors. I'm guessing she was sixty and, while her circumstances were now low, I could tell that a more genteel life had been lived in her past. I gave her coins when I had them as well as a couple of paintings I hoped she could sell. We called her Mme Beaufort.

She had told me she hated Americans; her daughter had been raped by soldiers in the war.

Unwed mothers after the war were considered a life form to ignore. The war was so few years ago in Paris, and many wounds were not healed. I mourned for Mme Beaufort and her daughter. It was not right for me to hide my identity behind secrecy. I'd never told her I was American. But that night, frightened by those military-style police, I needed to confess.

I told her I was American. "I've never before considered that Americans weren't always good guys." Sadness overwhelmed me.

After a pause, Mme Beaufort reached up to my chest and put her arms around me in an unexpectedly strong embrace. We wept together. She told me she never thought she would love an American. Along with Professor Du Boise, she became one of the best memories I have in my life.

That night in bed, I thought about Mormonism. When I was a preschooler, it had been fun to attend. My sister had subsequently joined the Church. That must make it okay. Maybe it could help me understand the sadness in the world. Today, I look back at myself as a hopelessly naive young man, to think the Church might help with sadness instead of creating it.

6.

Back to Mormonism

Life settled into a routine. I studied, painted, walked the city, and explored the galleries. I could buy little because I was poor. Professor Du Boise one day announced to me that he thought I was ready to sell my work. He took me to the Left Bank where many artists exhibited in stalls along the sidewalk that paralleled the Seine. In those days, both Parisians and tourists shopped there for original art pieces. One of the stall vendors, a friend of the professor's, looked at my work. He said he would try to sell it, keeping 50% for himself. My first painting sold that day.

Because of the professor, I now had a source of income. It was small at first, based in part on how many paintings I could complete. But the business grew. I was making money and could move to a safer area on the Boise de Boulong which reminded me of Central Park in New York. I was becoming more resident and less student.

James was true to his word and sent a loving letter every week, but each one was like being pulled away from a dream you were enjoying. I wanted to hear from him, of course I did ... but the dreamy Parisian days had nothing to do with a man building airplanes half a world away.

Gorgeous young men were everywhere in Paris, and the gay life was far more obvious than in America. That will happen when it isn't illegal. It was Professor Du Boise who spoke with me about sex or the lack of it.

"You have no lovers," he pronounced one day as we walked to the Left Bank. "Why is this?"

I stumbled around before blurting, "I'm a homosexual."

"But of course! I know this. I see you look at boys with the interest I want you to look at objects when you paint."

Because it was so unexpected, I laughed aloud. So did he.

"I have a lover in California. I am faithful to him."

"Americans! You are so strange with your customs. In France if you are hungry, you eat. If you are tired, you sleep. If you want sex, you have sex. No judgments." For him, it was as simple as that. It didn't mean I loved James less just because I wished to sample French goods. "But you do it in moderation. When you are hungry, you eat until you are full, then you stop. You don't overindulge. Sex is the same."

He told me where I could go to find people like myself. It was not long before I did. When I was hungry, I ate.

In gay Paris, many men used their initials, so I was WTC. I found men in the Moulin Rouge section of the city and occasionally brought one home with me. RS was younger, and he wanted more than I was willing to give ... my commitment to James kept me from beginning a meaningful relationship with anyone else.

* * *

I had another longing making itself known. I missed religion the fellowship and acceptance in a congregation. I had lost touch with the Church in my pre-teen days, after my mother kicked Gramma out of the house. Back in those days, I'd learned nothing about the Mormon stance on homosexuality. Even at eight, when I was baptized, perversity was not a subject on the kiddy study list. Continuing with the Mormon Church after Gramma left us was difficult for Jacquie and me. There wasn't one in our part of town. If we needed churchifying, we went to whatever was handy. Congregations were always friendly, warm, had songs to sing. But they weren't Mormon, the One True Church.

When James came into my life, I didn't know our lovemaking was perverse. I knew it was illegal in the US, but so was cohabitation by a man and woman who weren't married, at least in many states. In my mind, both straight and gay couples were "living in sin" according to the law.

James knew Mormons considered us an abomination long before I did; when he explained, I merely thought he meant they reflected society's opinion in general. He refused to go, and more than that, he refused to be gracious about me disappearing for a whole morning, one of only two we had off from work.

Now alone in Paris, religion began to niggle again. I believed in God, and I believed God was unhappy that I'd quit attending church. Things were going so well for me that I might owe Him a doff of my hat. Still, it was happenstance that pulled me back to a fellowship of any kind. It was the French Mormons who tried to straighten me out, both literally and figuratively.

A theater on the Champs-Élysées showed American films in English. I stood in line behind two guys speaking in English. They were wearing suits. I began to eavesdrop, a sport I love almost as much as football. They were Americans, both Mormon missionaries stationed in France. I introduced myself, explaining I had been baptized Mormon. They were Tom and Jerry. No kidding. Like three old buddies, we sat together to watch the movie. Afterwards, they gave me a card with the location of their Mormon church and the meeting times.

I went the next day. It was in the wealthiest part of Paris. I went in, wearing jeans. I had forgotten how formal the Mormons were at the time other churches were accepting that how you dressed had little to do with how you prayed.

It was a bit like being swept away by a tide. I was greeted and interviewed. I told them I was a student at the Sorbonne which was, at best, a half-truth. I was asked if I was an elder: no, I was only an ordained deacon (a role for boys younger than me). The churchman said he would order my records from the Church in Salt Lake City.

My French was good, better than his. At no point do I remember asking him to do such a thing. I was sucked back into the arms of that great institution. Within a week I was a member of the France congregation, given a Book of Mormon to study. I began attending Priesthood meetings and Sunday School. I felt warm and included, even though I had to call Tom and Jerry elders. I was fast-tracked past deacon on to elder status.

When asked if I was chaste, a requirement for the status, I said yes. I either had convinced myself that you could only be unchaste regarding a woman, or I told a flat out lie. When asked if I practiced any perversions, I said no. I didn't believe sex with a man was a perversion. It made no sense to me. What the bishops believed was perversity, I believed was natural. If God made me who I am, I reasoned, why couldn't God's Church accept that? The leadership must be mistaken, right? For a while, I kept my quandary to myself.

I was content. I had found religion with some kinks to work out, my painting was getting stronger all the time, I loved where I lived. The only hitch was James. Our plan was to get back together after my two years of school. I wrote to him that I wanted to stay longer, at least another year. I begged him to come. He wrote back, very upset with me. It wasn't so much the extra year as the fact that I decided it without consulting him. He was fifteen years older than me, and he was done waiting. I wrote that I was staying. No more letters arrived. Just like that, I destroyed his heart and mine.

Professor Du Boise was no real help. He saw me first and foremost as a young painter, exploring my skills. Of course, he thought I should stay.

I next went to the Mormon Church to explain my situation. I told them about James. The leadership was appalled. They, of course, told me homosexuality was all wrong. I was told the only way to save myself was to "find a fine woman, marry her, and raise a family." They said that when I experienced life with a good woman, all my feelings of gayness would go away.

Was it possible they were right? I could choose not to be gay by as simple an act as marriage? It didn't feel right.

But I believed them.

God help me, I believed them.

7.

"Au Revoir" to "I do"

I was twenty-six when I left France in 1962. My Parisian years after James were about painting, selling, and visiting other countries. My days were fun but empty. After so long, I missed my friends at home, especially my sister. And I believed I'd be coming right back to Paris, maybe with a fine woman as the Church instructed.

And before that, I knew I needed to find James to settle it. I couldn't accept that what he and I had shared was wicked. If he would still have me, I'm afraid that a fine woman would have to look elsewhere. If he wouldn't have me, then I would buckle down to the Church's advice. The love of the right woman would help me get over the loss of my first love. They said it, so it must be true.

My trip home was exceedingly tedious, a long return on the *Queen Elizabeth*, then trains to California. Without a storm at sea or cabins to clean − I could afford the trip without the sweat equity. I was bored. You really can't play shuffleboard with wealthy dowagers for five days in a row. Even the gigolos aboard didn't seem that interested in them.

I'd like to think that, instead of sulking through the whole stultifying trip, I studied the Book of Mormon or at least pondered the ways and whys of whom I was becoming. But, I was still young enough that the idea of serious reflection was not in my lexicon.

Young Me had a habit I didn't understand at the time. What extra money I made, I spent on dinners for my friends, or extra payments to Mme Beaufort, or alms for anyone who seemed to need them in all of France. You'll find this thread of generosity runs through the rest of my story; it explains many of the errors I make along the way.

I now realize why, since I *have* reached the age of reflection. Think back. I had no father, or at least I was banished from knowing who the real one was (assuming my mother even knew for sure, and I'd call that iffy). I could not understand why I wasn't loved. As a little boy, I was desperate to find affection, anything that would prove I wasn't merely one of life's errors. Surely, Young Me must have thought that people would like me if I was helpful, generous.

If I am a better boy, Daddy will come home to me. Mommy will love me.

This chronic need for love, approval, affection followed me the rest of my life. I didn't want to be a good employee, I wanted to be the best employee; I didn't want to be a good painter, I wanted to be a great painter; I didn't want to be a good lover, I wanted to be the finest lover. For approval, I was inclined to do what others suggested instead of what I wanted, which led to a pattern of reaching out only to be slapped back. But I kept reaching which, I guess, is either a sign I didn't have the sense to learn an obvious lesson, or I was a true believer in hope, a basic belief confirmed by the Mormon Church and alive within me. It was no small part of my dependence on such an august organization.

Jacquie's father, David, could have filled the Daddy role for me on the few occasions he came to see her, in the years before I went to grade school. But I was not his child. He barely tolerated me when he took me along with her to a movie, or better yet, a day on the Santa Monica Pier, riding the coaster, hearing a band concert, exploring the arcade, eating a marvelous thing called pizza. He took me because Jacquie insisted, or she wouldn't go. One of my earliest life lessons was to never underestimate the determination of my big sister. We stuck together like a roll of Gorilla Tape, nearly impossible to peel apart.

I looked to my mother's johns for the love of a father. This had the results you'd expect. Some of her regulars were kind to Jacquie and me, and I mis-indexed that kindness for affection more than once. One of them had a ranch, and he took us to ride his ponies. Another was a doctor whose affection, I think, was genuine. I told the neighbors he was my real father. One of them took it on himself to call the doctor's wife. He never came back, and the result was bruises on my fair skin the exact shape of my mother's red hairbrush.

* * *

When I emerged from the Los Angeles Station, California looked sun-baked and lurid after the softer color palette of Paris. I traveled light, leaving most of my possessions behind with Mme Beaufort; I intended to be back soon. All I needed to do in the US was see my sister, place my paintings in California galleries for a source of income, then bring my true love (male or female) back to the City of Light, in order to continue life on the Boise de Boulong, the Central Park of Paris.

I was met at the station by Jacquie and her husband, Dick. She was still the dark-eyed beauty that I had left six years ago. I'd grown taller, in fact was no longer a good-looking boy but a handsome man with a soft beard and what have been called knowing eyes. My big sister was now also my little sister, but her hug was as strong as ever. Dick eagerly welcomed me, too, so I felt at home living with them for a short time.

My first goal was to purchase a car. You didn't get around Southern California with a bike. While I had a better sense of fashion now ... or at least a bit more money to shop for new clothes vs. used ... I was not interested in wasting it on a vehicle fancier than I was. The third-hand 1956 Buick was so cavernous inside, it was damn near bigger than my first Parisian apartment.

I took Santa Monica Boulevard toward James's house. It was a slow route, but I wanted to smell California, feel the warmth, ingest the dry air. I needed to acclimate, if only to moderate the beat of my heart as my anticipation grew. I wanted James to be proud of the man I had become, a man who craved nothing so much as a second chance. Maybe James would be the true love who returned to Paris with me ... maybe I would not settle on a fine woman.

James didn't live there anymore. The people who did had no idea what became of him. I contacted our friends, but in truth, they'd always been more his than mine. If they knew, they weren't telling. I went to the bars where he'd been a drummer in his bands. Desperate, I even went to McDonnell Douglas. He'd worked there for years, but the personnel department had no idea where he'd gone. As I left, one guy from the parts department who'd known us both told me he'd heard that James was in Seattle, working at Boeing. But he wasn't sure it was true.

Hearts are strong, but mine was gutted that day. A small piece of it still yearns for this man who moved on, no doubt with someone else. He'd waited long enough. Some goddamn flight engineer at Boeing Field was in the bed that had been mine.

I mourned as I drove up the Coast to see our old haunts once more. Wind blasting through the car carried my howls out to the hills. I didn't want any other man but James. Finally drying to a snivel, I guessed that a woman couldn't make me feel any worse.

The following days did not improve my outlook. I was an artist. A Parisian artist who sold his work on the Left Bank. My credentials as an artist were a given. But California galleries did not respond to my magnificence. It was a rude discovery that they would not display my work without a hanging fee. In addition, I had to work in a shop to lower the forty percent fee for any sale. If that wasn't bad enough, the fact that my countrymen didn't demand originals (being happy with prints) finally broke me. It reminded me of my arrival in France, when I couldn't afford the paints for paintings.

Maybe my passion was no longer in it. It wasn't in much of anything. I couldn't afford to get back to Paris. It seemed the perfect time to join up and end it all in Vietnam. Even that failed; the military doctor said that asthma like mine would kill me before the Cong had a crack at me. I was rejected.

I had to find a job. General Telephone took me on, saving me from a diet of beans and rice (Top Ramen had not yet been introduced to the US market). I became a purchasing agent.

Rejection by James, galleries, and even the military slapped the joy out of me and turned me into just another working stiff.

For entertainment, I spent time with my Gramma. She was now in a nursing home, but maintained the firecracker personality that she'd always had. I adored her, and she me. Only Jacquie and I visited her; she was widowed and our mother had written her off long ago. I'm very glad of those last few visits with Gramma before she died, although she spent a large part of each visit ordering me to marry.

I hadn't found the woman who would light a fire so hot that perversion would burn right out of me. But I was actively seeking her. Jacquie came to the rescue. She'd come back to the Mormon Church while I was in Paris. She introduced me to her congregation, not mentioning that I was gay. She thought I needed community more than strife at that point in time. "We'll deal with all that later," she said. "After they know you, and want you in the congregation." As she was taught, she thought I could work it out with the help of a fine woman, and nobody needed be the wiser.

The Mormon Church in Santa Monica became my hunting ground. I met Marriage Prospect Number One at Sunday School. She was pretty, willing, and we quickly became engaged (it took about a month). After the engagement I discovered her drill-sergeant nature ... I was to march to her tune when and where she asked. In next to no time, I asked for my ring back.

Next was another Mormon girl. She was a tiny thing, sweet as a baby doll. We dated for two months, got engaged, and I broke it off a month later.

Prospect Number Three didn't stand a chance. By then, I realized that I might accept the idea of a wife, but not the reality. What was I to do?

About this time, one of the French missionaries I knew in Paris arrived at the Church in Santa Monica. He needed an apartment, and I needed to get out of Jacquie's and Dick's house. So the two of us got an apartment together. Does that sound like trouble to you?

The one-bedroom apartment had twin beds, and the missionary and I maintained that divide. We became close friends, often using the French familiar form to chatter away and keep in practice with the language. Another member of the congregation overheard and decided that, since we seemed so close, we must be gay.

The bishop called us into his office, like two bad school boys. I explained how we knew each other, and the missionary, in quite a snit, announced the whistleblower was wrong.

Still, there was an attraction, and we both knew it. He had never admitted to his interest in men, nor did he want to confront it. To preserve our friendship, it was time to part ways. Then and then only did we touch each other, just the once as a goodbye. I found another apartment for myself, and once again, egged myself on. I must find my fine woman pretty darn quick. (A side note: the missionary and I have recently continued our friendship through the miracle of social media. He remains a good God-fearing Mormon, with a very large, loving family).

My sparkplug of a sister nudged her husband Dick into introducing me to a woman from his office. He arranged a blind date for us.

"After all, what could go wrong? It's just a date to get you into the swing of things," Jacquie said. "She'll like you. Everybody likes you."

"Have a blast," Dick added. "Remember her name is Priscilla, but she hates it. Her nickname is Winkie."

"Winkie?"

"Some sort of Tiddlywinks champ as a kid. Don't screw it up."

I wondered if sailors who'd been shanghaied felt like I did. *The ship's a beauty, Matey, if you don't mind the shackles.* As though hearing a dirge, I drove the old Buick up to the Malibu mansion to meet Prospect Number Four.

A mansion, for the love of God. A mansion. And I couldn't afford paint. Great start to the evening. Thanks so much, Dick. Back then, his name didn't mean a dick, but I probably thought he was one, anyway.

A butler opened the door, lifted his nose into the air, and shooed me around to the back. I suppose he thought I was a delivery boy. The cook took me in. When I told her I was Winkie's date, she grinned like a gleeful jack-o-lantern, grabbed my hand, and nearly skipped back to the butler, to announce his blunder. I imagine she rarely had the chance to upset that particular applecart.

He apologized, asked me to please not tell the family, and took me to the front room where Winkie's parents were waiting to grill me. I could hardly tell them I was the son of a whore with an unknown father, and that I was suffering the loss of my gay lover. I dwelt more on my "education" at the Sorbonne, my success as an artist in Paris, my faith as demonstrated by my Mormon affiliation, and my budding career at General Telephone. By the time Winkie appeared, even I thought I was quite the catch ... maybe a career as a spin doctor would have been right for me.

Winkie might as well have been delivered to me on a cloud by unicorns. Prospect Number Four was, in fact, stunning. Angels sang as she entered the room. Her smile was aglow, Madonna-ish (I'm talking about the original one, not the singer). I was so wowed I didn't even squeal on the butler.

Our first evening, and many after that, were fun and carefree. We shared a love of movies and could outdo any other couple at charades. She rarely drank, nor did I. She taught me how to play tennis, and I explained the intricacies of football to her. We dated for a few months as I hemmed and hawed. I was not likely to find a more attractive girl than this one. We suited each other so well, our humor dovetailed, our desire to travel, our love of kids. I even thought she smelled divine!

I was aware that Winkie had been raised in luxury unlike any I had known. She wasn't lazy, and she held down a good job. But she didn't have a clue how to season an omelet or clean a toilet. I could teach her how to be a homemaker as she taught me how to be a Don Juan.

Still I dragged my feet. Finally, her mother and father announced they were taking their daughter and leaving town. All three looked very pointedly at me.

I should have told Winkie. I should have told her that I liked men, that the Church promised I'd leave that behind. I should have let her be part of my battle. But I didn't. I'd like to believe I had her welfare in mind, that I didn't want her to feel like a failure if it didn't work. But I don't remember seeing it through her eyes. It had to work. We wouldn't speak of it.

I bought yet another ring (I was by now the jeweler's best friend). Winkie and I sat in the capacious Buick in Santa Monica, watching a sunset and necking, as it was called in those days.

"I love you," I said.

"I love you!" she answered.

"Will you marry me?" Reveal ring.

"Phew! I thought you'd never ask."

"Of course, you'll have to become a Mormon."

"WHAT?"

"Well, I can't marry you if you don't convert. I thought that was understood." I had never discussed it with her, just assuming she'd be happy in a religion that demanded she obey her hubby.

Winkie agreed, although it took her Methodist parents awhile to look less appalled, hopefully not by me but by the conversion. Even though she agreed, we couldn't marry in an actual temple. A lower-on-the-totem-pole Mormon chapel took us in.

I can say without a bit of doubt that I loved Winkie. She'd gone well out of her way to do everything I asked, and I would have done the same for her. We spent our first night together in a fancy Santa Barbara hotel. We were both virgins, well, sort of. I'd never made love to a woman, other than the groping with Gracie after the prom. Winkie had never been with a man. The night was very gentle, a coming together of best friends. I suffered some confusion with the exact location of my target; I expected it to be somewhat higher to the front. She guided me off the taxi strip onto the runway with her hand.

I can't say it was blinding passion for me, but I enjoyed it. And Winkie wasn't shy about showing me what she needed. As we held each other, I was absolutely sure the gayness would soon drain away.

For our honeymoon, we drove to Seattle to visit the World's Fair. Seattle ... where James was rumored to have gone. Coincidence? Maybe.

Walking the fair, the underground, the old part of town, I think I watched for him everywhere. Apparently, gayness would take its own time to dissipate.

I had not yet mentioned to Winkie that my intent was to whisk her away to Paris someday. I couldn't afford it now, so what did it matter? She kept her job at an insurance company in Westwood, and I became a manager at General Telephone in Santa Monica. Together we brought in $16,000 per year. Even in the early sixties, that was meager. But her nesting instinct was strong, so we put on the yoke of a crippling mortgage; newlyweds are blind to risk. We bought a hovel in (where else?) Venice Beach. It was a couple blocks from the city dump. The two-bedroom bungalow was a long step down from the Malibu Mansion, but Winkie was happy. We skimped and had fun. I sold the old Buick, but not before christening that big back seat one wild night up the Coast. Winkie might not have been my first choice for such an episode, but she was a delightful choice. I had found my fine woman.

8.

Alpine Village

Mono Lake is nearly seven thousand feet up in the Sierra Nevada Mountains. Water couldn't drain out of it, so the lake grew alkaline. It's pretty enough, but it is also inhospitable to almost anything but alkali flies, brine shrimp, and the millions of migratory birds that feed on those shrimp and flies. Each year it disappoints dozens of would-be fishermen.

The town, Lee Vining, is named for the prospector who thought a salt mine would be a fine idea, back in the mid-nineteen hundreds. Today, millions of tourists pass by it on their way to the east entrance of Yosemite National Park. Very few spent time in Lee Vining in 1962. Gas stations, restaurants, and motels had a pretty hard-scrabble life. Most of the town closed due to snow long months of the year. It still has fewer than three hundred year-round residents who hunker down in the winter blizzards, like squirrels hibernating in a den. They scurry around in the drifts now and then, but mostly live off the nuts they've stored.

Why this geography lesson? Two tectonic plates were about to collide for my bride and me.

Plate One: After Winkie and I were married about six months, we were nearly out of money. The term "working poor" didn't exist in 1962, but that's who we were, proving once again that wise old adage, you can't live on love alone.

Plate Two: Winkie's parents, Helen and Roy, moved to Lee Vining shortly after our wedding. They had a beautiful home overlooking Mono Lake. Roy's favorite form of entertainment was to watch disappointed fishermen. To further entertain themselves in their retirement, they bought a gift shop in town. They wanted their daughter near them.

The Tectonic Collision: Helen and Roy bought an old motel for us to manage. In Lee Vining. Three hundred miles to the north and six thousand feet straight up from Venice Beach. They didn't ask, they just did it. I took it as a sign they were not happy with our life choices so far.

I didn't want to go. I could repair old buildings, sure, having lived in them all my life. But I was a beach boy who knew nothing about mountains and snow. If Winkie had agreed with me, I would have said no. However, she looked at the gesture as a loving wedding gift, not a pushy intrusion into our lives. She loved her parents and saw no reason to keep our distance. For her, this looked like the way out of a dire situation. It made sense. And I didn't have a leg to stand on. They offered a promising adventure; I offered insecurity.

I lectured myself that it was time I started thinking like a couple, instead of like a man on his own. I convinced myself it was the right thing to do. Winkie knew I would be a good provider in the future, and this was just the boost we needed. So I agreed. That's how a mama's girl with no idea how to clean became the maid at a motel. And how I, a painter of art, became a painter of walls.

We gave notice at our jobs, found a renter for our little house in Venice Beach, loaded up a U-Haul, and moved north, me with the joy of a chain gang. The motel was called Alpine Village which sounded jolly enough. Helen enthused that it had fifteen cabins to rent plus a separate house where we could live. As we drove north, Winkie and I tried viewing it as a new escapade, a chance to try our luck in the burgeoning new hospitality industry.

"We can become rich!" Winkie assured me.

"It will be fun!" I assured myself.

In order to avoid bogging down in tears, I believe I'll tackle our three Alpine Village years one issue at a time.

ISSUE ONE: FIXER-UPPERS

As you have no doubt guessed, the place was a disaster. When someone in Lee Vining is done with a piece of real estate, it's time to call the rag man. On first sight I said to Winkie, "Gosh. I hadn't realized California was bombed in the war." I loaned her my handkerchief to wipe her tears.

On the upside, the two-story house was still erect even if the angle was jaunty. And I was quite used to the shack lifestyle, although it was a mind-blowing experience for Winkie. I soon had electricity and plumbing working again, as long as nobody got too fussy about codes.

My main concern was getting the fifteen cabins rentable. We had no source of income until that happened. I looked at each unit as a gremlin waiting to destroy me. I painted walls and roofs. I dug holes under them to get at the plumbing in order to fix it. I knew the day would come when I needed to add foundations to them all, but I bypassed that step for now. Meanwhile I glazed windows, repaired doors, patched flooring. Roy's third favorite form of entertainment was to sit back and cheer me on.

Winkie learned to sew curtains and bedspreads. She disinfected the mattresses, sprinkled them with baking soda, and vacuumed them once, then did it again. She developed a certain amount of artistry with throw rugs, and absorbed all there was to know about cleaning toilets and wallpapering. In time, each little gremlin became rent-worthy, but it never stayed that way. One caught fire, one threw me off the roof, one flooded even though the area was dry as a bone. It was like being haunted by fifteen miniature Hill Houses, each of which was out to kill us. Winkie and I were exhausted day and night. But we started to earn a living. We paid Helen and Roy their pound of flesh each month. Of course, our first blinding snow shut us down for the next six months.

ISSUE TWO: SEX AND THE MORMON CHURCH

No matter how exhausted young marrieds may be, there is still enthusiasm for sex ... even when both would prefer a male partner. We had three babies during our three years in Lee Vining, two of them appearing as twins. I was manning up. There was no Mormon Church anywhere near us to keep me on track. Fortunately, temptation stayed a long way away; there was no colony of homosexual mountain men in the immediately area.

I was very anxious for my gayness to dissipate, as I was assured it would. It did not seem to be happening. Winkie and I had both grown strong and lost weight during our enforced labor. We were in incredible physical shape. She could not have been more stunning. And I really tried. But something was missing for me: a man. I could function, but I wasn't attracted.

I found that the easiest way for me to achieve a hard-on was to imagine I was with a man. This felt seedy; I was as guilty as a boy caught with porn and his pants down. When would the gayness begin to give way, and make sex with a woman a complete pleasure?

Meanwhile, as my interest waned, hers waxed. I started having nights that I was "too tired" or "had a headache." Winkie was having none of it; she loved the challenge. Who was this vixen in my bed? She would force me down and climb aboard to ride like the wind. Frankly, the aggressor stuff actually worked. It was better for me and better for her when she decided on the rules of the game. And like I mentioned before, it did result in babies which thrilled us both.

ISSUE THREE: IN-LAWS

Roy was a good old boy, and we did well enough together as long as I mowed his lawn and laughed at his jokes. But Helen, wow. I guess her daughter had to learn aggression from someplace. Helen held our money, doing the books and telling us how much we had left after the lion's share went toward the debt incurred when they purchased Alpine Village. I never knew the financials and was considered inappropriately intrusive when I asked. If we ate out, she made sure I felt like a helping hand allowed a seat due to the largesse of the master.

In the three years as a motel entrepreneur, I remember spending "fun" money on ourselves only once. A couple, Alicia and Darin, came from San Francisco to visit us. They'd tour Yosemite during the day, and we'd go out at night. We went to a topless bar a long way out of town; none of us had ever been to one, and it sounded seriously wild. The wives dared each other to go. After the fact, I told Winkie she had the best equipment in the place, which earned me a brilliant smile. That outing was one of the few secrets Winkie ever kept from her mother. My secret, of course, was that I would have preferred male strippers.

The next day, Darin got stuck walking in quicksand in Mono Lake. I pulled him out, but he lost his shoes in the process. He bought moccasins from Helen's gift shop which was the only time that she didn't treat our guests like a lesser species.

As I reread this, it sounds like I didn't much like Helen.

ISSUE FOUR: WORK, WORK, WORK

Each winter when the Tioga Pass shut down, Lee Vining rolled up its sidewalks. We closed the motel and headed to Oakland or San Francisco where I found work for the winter. Westinghouse was a wonderful employer, hiring me more than once as a purchasing agent.

A co-worker one winter was a new file clerk named Janis Joplin. One and the same. She was a whiz and soon had everything filed that her predecessor had left strewn about. However, about a month after she started, nobody could find anything. Turns out Janis caught up quickly by merely putting the paperwork in random drawers in whatever file she found. She was fired, but her replacement was a lot less fun. As a file clerk, Janis was a great singer.

Back in Lee Vining each spring, I added more jobs to that of motel manager. I worked nights in a gas station, clerked at a market, broke down chunks of pumice from the volcanoes in the area. My boss paid me based on the number of baskets I could fill with the rock. Neither Winkie nor I wanted to be any deeper in her parents' debt.

Then a minor miracle happened. Our renters in Venice Beach moved out. *Damn it,* I thought. *Who else would want a tinderbox close to the city dump?* What I didn't know was that the dump had been dredged and Marina del Rey created. Realtors began bidding on the house. I sold it for three times what I had paid. Now we had a little money of our own, just in case. This tiny bit of daylight felt like freedom.

ISSUE FIVE: BABIES!

In the summer of 1965, our twin boys were born. They were so fragile, just a little over three pounds each. I wanted a far better childhood for my children than I'd had for myself. I needed to be the father I'd never known. But I was still shocked by the outpouring of emotion when I first met those squalling preemies. Doug and Jeff. It was as if I had grown two new nerves, parts of myself now open for the world to batter about.

When they cried, my heart broke. When they hungered, my stomach rumbled. We were one. I craved tiny Superman shields to protect them always.

It was over a month before we could bring them home. That gave me time to make room in our two-bedroom house, to sanitize and soften in preparation for doubling the number of residents. Winkie and I were as happy as a couple of helium balloons, flying high.

Life was sweet for a while. I had my first snapshot of how intertwined family life should be. Winkie cleaned the cabins during the day while I watched the kids and did chores. She checked people in through the afternoon while I slept. All night I worked at the gas station across the street, keeping an eye on our house. Winkie came over with dinner and the babies in the early evenings when the cabins were full, so we could grab a few minutes together. Then they went home to bed.

Helen rarely helped. Neither she nor Roy were interested in babysitting or other grandparent things. In fact, when Winkie went into labor with our daughter, Laura, the next summer, I called Helen to come watch the boys. She said she needed to shower, fix her hair, and do her make-up before she left home. In a panic, I corralled a willing neighbor into taking the boys before I loaded Winkie and left for the hospital, which was many miles away.

That ended our time in Lee Vining. I was dead tired of the constant moving in the winters, but mostly I wanted away from the in-laws. They never shared any of the money we put into the motel. And I never depended on my mother-in-law again.

Winkie, two one-year-olds, a baby, and I headed back to Southern California.

9.

South of the Border

With money from selling our Venice Beach house, Winkie and I rented an apartment in Santa Monica. We put the babies in three cribs in one bedroom, and we took the other. The living room looked like a used toy store ... it was a decorating style we would employ for several years to come. Other families lived in the apartments around us so nobody complained about crying babies or stuffed animals in the hall or Huffy trikes on the sidewalk. We were welcomed to the building by a barbecue complete with burgers, gelatin molds, and pineapple-upside-down cake.

I needed to look for work, but another duty wedged itself in first. Trouble was brewing for my sister Jacquie, trouble that had started before we left Lee Vining.

A refresher: Jacquie had left our mother's little house of horrors to marry Dick. Dick had introduced me to Winkie. The four of us became friends.

Dick, Jacquie, and their baby Craig came to visit us at Alpine Village shortly before we moved back to Southern California. We put them in the cabin that was least likely to try to kill them.

When Jacquie and I had time to be alone, walking a trail near Mono Lake, she broke down and sniffled out a story about gross infidelity. Dick, who worked in Los Angeles, had stopped coming home each evening, leaving Jacquie with the baby and no means of transportation. He'd say he was working late, sometimes overnight. Jacquie's fears were confirmed when one of Dick's ex-girlfriends called her to spill the beans. It appeared that Dick was well-advanced in this "unfaithful" stuff since he was being unfaithful to his girlfriends as well as his wife. I'd known Dick for a long time, but had no idea of any of this. I guess a guy doesn't tell his wife's brother what extramarital arrangements he's making.

Jacquie was distraught, but had not yet confronted Dick; you can credit her baby brother at this point with keeping her from confronting him with a butcher knife. As we walked back to the cabin, discussing her options, a car pulled in the Alpine Village drive. It was my friend Bruce with his wife, Jill, who were spending a couple nights with us. I gave them the cabin second-least likely to terrorize the occupants.

So on one side, Bruce was joyfully telling me about his new affiliation with the Church of the Firstborn. On the other side, my sister was having a meltdown. I was a ping pong ball, trying to match moods as I was paddled back and forth.

At last, Jacquie, Dick, Craig, Bruce, and Jill all left for their homes. In a moment of silence that followed, Winkie patted my arm and said, "At least Bruce and Jacquie seem to get along. She can use a friend now." Winkie's antennae picked up what I did not.

Soon thereafter, we moved to Santa Monica. Looking for work and setting up a household were my priorities. I admit, Jacquie's drama slipped to the recesses of my mind. Until the phone rang.

"Bruce and Jill have been living with me off and on. I'm liking the sound of their new church," Jacquie said as soon as she identified herself.

This was a jaw-dropping surprise. Bruce's church, the Church of the Firstborn, was a disavowed offshoot of the Mormons.

Jacquie wasn't done. "I'm leaving Dick and moving to Mexico with baby Craig. Bruce's parents have a house there where I can stay."

Jacquie? This was Jacquie? Salt-of-the-earth, logical Jacquie who had fought my battles, wiped my butt, navigated me through childhood? Who was this wild female?

"Ja-Jacquie!" I sputtered. "Bruce's married! You're married! Have you thought this ... "

"I'm not marrying Bruce, dopey. Just moving with him and Jill to Mexico."

"But what about Dick?"

"Wait'll he finds out I've taken Craig to Chihuahua to live." I believe my big sister actually cackled.

"Chihuahua? To a colony of polygamists?" Many Mormons had colonized in this Mexican state where they could still make merry with multiple wives.

"That has nothing to do with it."

Oh, well, that certainly clarified everything. I drove to Simi Valley to talk with her. When I got there, she was frantically packing. Dick hadn't been home for two days, and Bruce was on his way to pick her up. I pleaded with her to take some time, think this through. Jacquie was triumphant in her decision, and I was a wreck.

I kissed baby Craig goodbye. Bruce, Jill, and Jacquie waved as the car pulled away, and I stood there alone. Jacquie had promised she'd call me if she needed my help. I went home to Winkie and stewed for a week. "I have to know," I finally burst out. "I have to find her, be sure she is okay." Winkie, bless her, agreed I should go; she knew how close Jacquie and I were.

I wrote to Jacquie to ask for directions to come visit. While I awaited a reply, I found employment in Los Angeles with a wholesaler of electrical pole line hardware; they coveted my experience as a purchasing agent with Westinghouse. I told them it would be a couple weeks before I could start, and they agreed. Knowing a job awaited me eased the worry about leaving my family. Besides, friends who lived in the apartment complex said they would keep an eye on Winkie and the kids.

A letter arrived from Jacquie saying she was fine. She sent directions to her Mexican location via Texas. Then she closed with an arcane warning about not leaving El Paso after 3 p.m. on any afternoon.

Was my sister going crazy? Maybe. Later that week I received a call from Dick; she hadn't told him she was going ... or where. His poor attendance at home meant he didn't know she was gone until, I don't know, maybe he needed his laundry done.

"She took our son and disappeared!" he howled. I handled the situation with aplomb, saying I couldn't imagine such a thing and had no idea where she was. I didn't mention I'd been at his house when she left with Bruce and Jill, baby in tow. Oh what a tangled web we weave.

I left our car for Winkie and headed off in a Rent-A-Wreck with road maps of Arizona, Texas, and Mexico. I went from Santa Monica through Phoenix and slept in a Lucky Supermarket parking lot for a few hours in Tucson. The next day I had a burger and fries for lunch in El Paso, then I headed down Highway 2 into Mexico. I had completely forgotten Jacquie's warning to not leave later than three o'clock.

It was another few hours to Nuevo Casas Grandes. A century or so earlier, Mormons in Conestoga wagons rolled into Mexico so they could continue to practice polygamy. In fact, the town looked beautiful, a lot like Mormon communities in the US. A lot of the colonies failed, but the one in Nuevo Casas Grandes, Chihuahua had grown as a robust agrarian society. Jacquie's dad had been born here. As I passed through town, I wondered if she had looked for his home.

The location of Bruce's house was still quite a long drive ahead, so I continued on into the dusk. I was about to discover why Jacquie had warned me against coming this way late in the day. I was tired and the drive seemed endless. About twenty miles south of a town called Galeana, I saw a truck blocking the road ahead. I slowed. Another truck pulled up behind me. I was trapped.

Men from the first truck walked toward me, guns in their hands. My stomach turned cartwheels; my mouth opened for a silent scream, I instantly needed to pee. They made me get out and forced me to hand over my wallet and any cash I had in my jeans. I thought they would kill me then. Who would help Winkie raise our babies? My silent scream came out at last as a mournful cry.

Instead of shooting me, the men tied my hands behind my back and lifted me into the bed of their pickup. I was pushed over on my side; I could see nothing of what we might be passing. But being tied up was a good thing, right? Bad guys don't tie up people before they shoot, do they?

The drive did not seem long to me. When I got out of the truck, I noticed one of the men had driven my Rent-A-Wreck off the road behind us and into a ramshackle collection of sheds. I felt happy for the Rent-A-Wreck people ... shock makes your brain function like a Wiffle ball, bouncing every which way. The banditos dragged me into a hovel and tied me to a wooden chair.

"Where are you heading, Señor?" one asked me in English. He was willowy as a track star while the other three had been eating too many tacos.

Amazing how that simple question, which didn't involve the removal of any of my body parts, eased my mind. He spoke my language and was interested in my journey! You don't murder people you're interested in. "My sister lives in La Ciudad de los Santos. A Mormon colony. I'm visiting her. And loving the scenery of Mexico, what a wonderful place you have here."

Track Star was not into compliments. "Her name?"

I told him, hoping Jacquie was still using Dick's last name.

"You are safe, Señor, if your sister is smart." He didn't quite smile, but his eyes weren't cruel. Did I have Stockholm Syndrome already?

He left. I was glad that events so far hadn't literally scared the piss out of me, because I usually try for a shred of dignity. But I desperately had to go now. One of the men untied me and pushed me into an empty chicken coop. I immediately pissed on a wall. Then I asked a guard for water, mimicking drinking from a glass. He obliged with a used paper cup from Taco Bell, filled with warm water. It was delicious. You don't give water to a man you are about to torture with a screwdriver or bludgeon with a jack handle. A man doesn't refuse it based on its questionable cleanliness, either.

Chicken coops in general have no chairs, and this was no different. I sat on the dirt floor in the dark. Exhausted, I finally tipped over and lay prone. They hadn't hurt me, but they hadn't worried themselves about my comfort. I was dirty, sweaty in heat that did not abate as the moon rose, listening to international creepy crawlies shuffle over and around me through the night. In the distance, dogs howled. I prayed they were merely dogs.

I took stock of my circumstances. On the upside, I reasoned, if they hadn't killed me yet, maybe they wouldn't. And I'd never heard of a slave trade in white men; usually white men were on the better end of those deals. I finally drifted off, putting my brain out of its misery for a few hours.

Protesting muscles and joints brought me back to life. In the fullness of time, the men awoke, and one took me to an outhouse. If your captors allow you to dump, they probably aren't going to kill you. Back in my coop, they provided more water but no food. Much more of that water probably *would* have killed me.

The gang took off mid-morning, leaving one guard. As the sun climbed and heated the sky past the sizzle point, he drifted off to sleep. I began to explore the back wall of the coop and found a loose board.

I know this sounds like a bad TV show, but what can I say?

I pulled off two loose boards and quietly crept out. I executed a stealthy crawl, my belly glued to the ground. When I was exhausted, I raised myself enough to bound forward in a bent-over position. Finally, I stood up and ran out of the drive and across the road to the dry ditch beside the roadbed. Nobody followed, at least not yet.

Scraped and sore, I gathered my breath then began jogging down the raised crest of the road. It was totally still; I would hear a truck coming before I saw it, and I could dive back into the ditch before they saw me. I headed in the direction of La Ciudad de los Santos, thinking it must be closer and safer than retracing my steps to Galeana.

I was so hungry and dehydrated, I couldn't jog for long. I slowed to a walk and continued through the afternoon. I wanted to hitch a ride but there was no traffic, and when I did hear something coming, it was roaring at great speed. I leaped off the road to hide. For a time, trucks raced back and forth, and then they were gone.

That night I hid under the road in a dry culvert. By morning, I knew I was in serious trouble. Rattlers, tarantulas, Gila monsters, scorpions? None of those poison boys seemed as dangerous as going any longer without water. If I had to confront the banditos, so be it. I climbed up onto the road and waited.

I have no idea why the American couple stopped for the crazy man in the Chihuahua emptiness. I was parched; they gave me water and an RC Cola. I was famished; they gave me half an olive loaf sandwich, a bunch of grapes, and a Bit-O-Honey from their small store of provisions. I stunk of filth and sweat; they never once complained. I needed a ride; they took me to La Ciudad de los Santos. I can only hope that goodness and mercy followed them the rest of their days.

The colony called La Ciudad de los Santos had a checkpoint. When Jacquie was told I was there, she came running; she feared I was dead. She took me to Bruce's and Jill's house. They let me shower, and Bruce gave me a set of clothes. He escorted me to a local store that had a phone so I could call Winkie, then we returned to his house where Jill and Jacquie served a large lunch. I quickly told them what had happened, then I stuffed my face with *arroz con pollo*. It could have been rice and *pelicano* for all I cared. I was famished.

"Your banditos kept us pretty busy, too, you know," Bruce said.

"Mgffrg?" I managed while still chewing.

"Yes. Your sister and I were quite the Bonnie and Clyde."

Jacquie said, "They turned up here looking for me. They said they were holding you for ransom."

"Gave us your driver's license to prove it." Bruce held it up and handed it back to me. "They returned the rental car, too. No wallet though."

Between them, they told me the rest of the story. They followed the outlaws to the compound where I was held. Bruce said, "I had the money to pay them ... they didn't think you were worth much, if I'm honest with you."

Well, fuck them, I thought, still shoveling in the chow.

"When we got there, you were gone. They were furious," Jacquie said.

"I knew something was wrong so I turned the car around, hit the gas, and headed back down the highway."

"They followed and started shooting at us! I was crying because I thought you were dead. Bruce told me to open the glove box."

"I always keep a pistol in there. Just in case."

Now there's the ol' Mormon spirit! I thought.

Jacquie nodded. "I got it out, leaned way out the window, and I shot back at them!" Her eyes glistened. "I must have surprised them or hit something important. At least the truck swerved off the road and tipped over into the ditch."

"Feisty sister you have here," Bruce said, smiling at Jacquie. "But that was two days ago. We all thought you must be dead."

"Now here you are!" Jacquie said with a laugh. "And you thought you had to keep me safe. I'd say you were the one in danger! Not me, little brother."

At that very moment, a boy appeared at the door to say a man named Dick was asking for Jacquie at the checkpoint.

So far, my trip to Mexico had not been particularly pleasant. Bruce pointed out the home of the colony's host, and told me to take Dick there. I walked down to the checkpoint to meet my brother-in-law.

Dick was beside himself. He was so furious at Jacquie, he didn't even ask what I was doing there.

"I don't want her back, but I want my son," he shrieked.

I told him I would take him to the house where Craig and Jacquie lived. If he had been in his right mind at all, he'd have known that couldn't be true; I'd never betray my sister that way.

When we reached the house, three Hulk-sized teenagers appeared at the door. They grabbed Dick and told him to leave town or he would be hurt. I suspect they did hurt him some as they dragged him back to the checkpoint and sent him on his way. I was quite flustered, but the host of the commune told me to stay behind. He gave me a gun, suggesting I shoot Dick if he returned. "Don't worry, son," he said. "We'll bury him in the wilderness where he'll never be found."

What the hell?

This colony was as crazy as the banditos! Kill Dick? I would never shoot my brother-in-law! I sat there stunned. When I finally could, I stood, put the gun on the table in the middle of the host's living room, and left his house.

Dick was gone. Jacquie wanted to stay. Period. In less than a day, I'd outstayed my welcome in La Ciudad de los Santos Colony. I was beginning to feel in as much danger from the Mormons as the Mexicans; each was outside my idea of the law. My beloved sister would be lost to me for many years to come as she folded into this religious cult. She did marry Bruce, as did three more women after her.

In sorrow, I left the following morning with two of those husky teenagers driving cars to the front and to the back of the Rent-A-Wreck. Maybe they were keeping me safe from banditos, or maybe they were making sure I left the country and the colony behind. Either way, I crossed the border back to El Paso long before three o'clock in the afternoon.

10.

San Bernardino

"If Jacquie doesn't want to leave the colony, then you should let her live with that decision," Winkie said when I returned from Mexico. At the time, she was nursing the baby, and I was wiping breakfast glop from the faces of both boys. I know she was glad I was home. Wrangling three babies was no easy chore.

Like her mother, Winkie was quick to form opinions and hard to rattle out of them. So for a time, the subject was closed. And what was there to discuss anyway? That my sister was an idiot? That I should hire mercenaries to steal her away? That I was reluctant to repeat my experience in a chicken coop any time soon?

Winkie had news for me she was eager to share. "Bill and Polly are moving. The owner offered their apartment to us if we maintain the complex. I jumped at the chance." So, we were back in the real estate management business. A handful of apartments sounded far more rewarding than fifteen malevolent little cabins. And our new digs were far bigger, with three bedrooms and two baths.

After the move, I began work for the LA company that sold electrical pole line hardware. I found the job a good fit to my skills; I was organized and knowledgeable regarding the needs of wholesale customers, so clients were happy with me. A contact at General Electric suggested I interview with them. They offered more money and benefits. I took the job. That's how my twenty-year stint with GE began.

I drove into LA from Santa Monica each morning, early to avoid traffic. In the 1960s, Southern Cal roads were already a zoo. I listened to the Boss Radio jocks at KHJ as I sipped a cup of coffee and weaved lane to lane. Coffee was a pleasure I hid from Winkie and the other Mormons in my sphere of friends. I may have given up men for the Church, but early morning java was too much to ask.

I scurried into work by 6 a.m. most days. My East Coast suppliers were three hours ahead time-wise, and I wanted to have pricing settled and orders filled before West Coast offices opened. By the time my LA customers arrived at their desks, they were already supplied for their day. The regional manager asked me if I could handle more. Ever eager, I said of course, if they paid overtime. He agreed.

Before long, I was offered the position of operation manager in the San Bernardino office.

More pay, more prestige, moving expenses. I was thrilled. I was becoming a mogul and had only just begun! For the next twenty years, GE moved me from San Bernardino to Anaheim to Santa Clara, each time with a larger office and more responsibility.

In San Bernardino, we flourished. Winkie and I bought our dream home, a palace to me. I have seen it since and realize it was nothing all that special. But at that time, it was the sign of my arrival from the basest kind of squalor. It graced the side of a green hill where the children played. They could walk to grade school safely.

We lived the American dream for many years. We were a good team, raising happy kids and enjoying each other and worshipping as Mormons. Gayness had not left me, but other priorities simply mattered more. As much as I liked being a dependable breadwinner and cherished husband, I loved time with my children. Our kids never doubted their parents' commitment to their welfare, at least not when they were little. They had our attention, all the support they could want, and an adoring if dimwitted Irish setter named Kelly. These were the halcyon days of my life, when storms didn't rage and all was calm.

The biggest dangers my little boys faced were some of the Little League parents. I believed it was only a game; they believed the boys must win. One father even approached me for a fight or duel or shoot out; I don't know because we didn't get that far. When I stood up, and he saw how beefy I was, he turned on his heel. This is the only crime story I have from my years in San Bernardino. We had far better luck with Boy Scouts than Little League; both my sons went on to be Eagle Scouts in high school. I was so proud of them. Still am, for that matter.

From the beginning of the school years, it was important to Winkie and me that the boys were not in the same class; we didn't want them competing with each other. Twins should develop their own identities, we believed, although both of them intentionally befuddled the teachers with who was who when it served their purpose.

Life was stable, and for the first time I felt settled. I believed that my gay days were finally behind me. I put Paris out of my mind and knew that painting was no option when raising a family.

My bond with the Mormon Church grew stronger, as did Winkie's. We started attending chapel weekly while living in San Bernardino. Sometimes, we went to the temple in Santa Monica. The kids attended their Sunday School, and we went to ours. In time, I taught a class, became a leader for the Elders Quorum, took responsibility for overseeing young adults. These were fulfilling years for us as we ascended in stature in the eyes of the congregation. I spent many hours each week in worship or helping others find their way. My natural inclination to be giving was a boon; I felt good about myself. I was an asset to the Mormon Church.

Bishop Gregory became my closest friend. We worked well together, shared a love of art, movies, football. I trusted him enough to finally tell him I fought homosexuality, and that the French Mormons had said I could get it out of my system with a proper relationship. Gregory supported their viewpoint, kept my secret, and applauded my efforts. He believed that a man could conquer these feelings, and that I was trying hard enough that I would succeed. We trusted each other. It is a great sorrow for me, the rough times we put each other through before this story ends. But for now, we were friends, my family was happy, and my job was a good one. With all that contentment, something just had to go wrong.

A new family moved into the ward, an elder named Carl, his wife, and their three youngsters. I went to welcome them, and found him to be a likeable man with a good idea but no finances to develop it. Carl wanted to build and run a concessions business at the county fairgrounds. He needed start-up capital.

The venture would require several stands to serve the entire fifty-acre area. It was far more than a fair ground, encompassing live performances at Swing Auditorium, a football arena, an auto track, and an area for swap meets. Each area needed one or two concession stands. We would manage them all, although they wouldn't all be open at the same time, depending on the events on the grounds.

I had the money, was willing to invest, and thought it sounded like fun to work on Saturdays, reserving Sundays for Church. I worked at the counter of the busiest stand each weekend, handled clean-up, restocked, even learned to man the grill. If other GE employees spotted me there, it delighted them to see the boss flipping burgers. Our business of brats and fries, sodas and beer began to jump. We loved the entertainment, too, seeing games, races, rock concerts, you name it. Bob Hope wasn't all that funny, but I thought Elvis was great.

I loved football. I played it as a kid and have been a fan ever since. I'd often go high into the stands to watch the game, then run back down to work in the concession booth by halftime. One night, I saw a young man turn around to look up at me. He did it again. Then again. I looked behind me to see what was going on. Nobody was there.

This guy was flirting with me. It had been a long time since I'd been anywhere that a handsome man could show interest ... either that or my radar for such things was turned off by my idealistic married life. Whatever, I felt warmed by the attention, even though I fought the impulse to flirt back.

I left the stands and went to our concession booth at halftime. The dark-haired, bearded flirt followed and bought a beer, showing his ID to

Carl but looking at me as I worked. At least he wasn't a teenager. And just because you may be questioning it, yes we sold beer. The Mormon rule is that we can't *drink* cola or beer. Carl and I chose not to ask the Church any more about it.

After the game I cleaned the booth, as usual. Carl left with the money to drop at the bank on his way home. It took me an hour to scrub the stand, store our supplies, and put food into our walk-in freezer. When I went to the parking lot, it was virtually empty. Except for this guy. He was out there waiting for me.

The concessions business put me on display, in the right place to meet the wrong kind of strangers. I'd like to say I didn't enjoy it. But, my oh my, when I saw that handsome stranger waiting for me, you better believe the old Wayne was back.

I was mortified! According to the Church this would not happen. I'd been turning the other cheek, so to speak, for years, burying my true desires deep inside. All of a sudden my feelings of gayness came roaring back like a king tide. I tried to deny it. My mouth said the right words, but my body didn't listen.

He said his name was George.

I said, "I have to get home to MY WIFE AND KIDS."

He smiled.

"I am leaving now to spend the evening with my FAMILY and GO TO THE MORMON CHURCH in the morning."

He smiled.

"I have to set up at THE SWAP MEET first thing so I must go now."

I knew what he had in mind, and it excited me. It messed with my brain. It stirred up my desire. I was having feelings that were supposed to be gone. The Church had promised! I wasn't to blame ... was I?

George showed up at the swap meet, looking tanned, buff, delicious. I assured him I was not interested. But I gave myself over to self-pity and anger about the unfairness of it all. I loved my children. I loved my wife. But for years, I'd given up my true nature to work like a dray horse. I'd given up painting; I'd given up Paris; I'd given up James. The Mormon promise had not come true; the feeling of gayness had not gone away. It was baloney to call it a "feeling." It was a solid, cold fact of my existence. This desire, so natural and elemental, could not possibly be perverse.

What would it be like to have sex again with a man?

11.

Hitting Bottom

It was September of 1977 when my affair with George began. Winkie and I had been married sixteen years. Our twins, Doug and Jeff, were twelve and little Laura a year younger.

Of course I was guilty. What I was doing was wrong even in my own mind. I tried to convince myself that other men had affairs all the time. Straight men cheated on their wives. My mother made a career out of servicing married men; my brother-in-law had been unfaithful to my sister. What I was doing was immoral, okay, but I didn't see that my choice of a male vs. a female made it any worse. I was to discover that Winkie strongly disagreed with this.

George and I established a pattern. He lived in an apartment I visited in the mornings on my way to work. Our affair thrived for a couple of years; I even became close to his siblings. He wanted me to leave Winkie, but I was resolute that I wouldn't do that.

Still, I lied to her and cheated on her for two years. I'm guilty as charged of being a chump. George was the most exciting sexual partner I'd had in years, but I hated the subterfuge and untruths. The angst over the situation took its toll on me. I was only in my early forties when I ended up hospitalized with a heart issue that plagues me to this day.

The situation couldn't last, and it didn't. One fateful day, when I came home from an outing with the boys, Winkie told me George's sister had called. He'd been in an auto accident and was in a Riverdale hospital, asking for me.

"Who's George?" Winkie asked, voice cold as stone.

"I'll tell you when I get home," I said, galloping from the house. If you ever find yourself in a similar situation, I suggest you prepare a better way to handle it.

George was in terrible shape, muttering, "Wayne, I love you." His family made room for me to sit with them. I ached for him, so fragile and broken from his run-in with a car. But he would recover, or so the medical experts told us.

By the time I went home, my marriage needed an ICU of its own. Winkie was smart. She'd put things together, but she didn't believe it. She was in shock.

I confessed then. It was worse than she feared. This was no drunken one-night stand or burst of curiosity. This was a two-year affair that involved loving a partner other than her. A male partner. I thought I might use that in my defense. "It wasn't another woman, honey."

She went from tears to fury. "You think that would make it better, you idiot? For eighteen years, you tricked me. I was never the person you wanted. Eighteen years you've made a fool of me. Everything has been a lie."

She stormed away from me, slamming the door to our room.

I sat outside our bedroom door and cried. "Everything has not been a lie. I love you, I love our kids."

She yelled one last thing. "I'm ashamed for believing in you. Go away."

She was right, of course. From her point of view, the affair had begun all those years ago; by not telling her the truth before we married, I'd been unfaithful all of our lives. Her life was broken. Who could blame her if she left me? But the thought scared the hell out of me.

When she came out a couple hours later, I was beside myself with worry. It's like a different person walked into the living room. She had composed herself, but not with intent to make it easy on me. Whatever love she possessed for me had curdled. "I won't leave you because the Church will blame me, that I wasn't woman enough to fill your needs."

"Oh, Winkie, that's not . . ."

"Shut up. The kids are not to know."

"I would never ..."

"Shut up. This is up to you to solve, Wayne."

Spinning on her heel and heading for the kitchen, she turned her back on me. Even though we'd try to continue a life together, she never really turned back to me again.

I went to see George. I found him in his apartment, in bed with another man. Are you keeping track? I had an affair with a man who had an affair with another man while I was trying to make things right with my wife. Would I have left her if George had remained available? I'd like to say a resounding no. But I can't be sure.

I told Winkie I would go to the Church for guidance. As a Mormon herself, she believed in its ability to cast aside this perversion. She wanted to shame me; she had that right. Having to confess to my closest friend, Bishop Gregory, certainly accomplished that goal. He was, of course, shocked. He thought I was in control, that I had been saved by family and church.

"I thought so, too," I said. I was miserable, on the brink of losing both my wife and my best friend. Yet, something within me fought back. "It is not a problem that will go away, Bishop," I sobbed. "Either the Church is wrong, or it is not being truthful about homosexuality as a natural occurrence in God's flock."

Wrong? Untruthful? He was further shocked by such an explosion. To call the Mormon Church such evil things was further sacrilege.

"Bishop, I have tried," I pleaded. "I love my family. I've been faithful to one wife for sixteen years. There are many men in this Church that can't say that. Polygamists, even. Desiring males is as natural to me as desiring females is to them."

Bishop Gregory was rattled but resolute. He wanted to protect his friend, no matter how wayward I had become. But the Church had to know. He thought it would be lenient due to my confession and to my long service. He was wrong. The Mormon Church put me on trial and excommunicated me. I could no longer speak in meetings, I was no longer a leader of anything, I could not take the Sacrament. For all practical purposes, I was shunned by everyone.

Winkie and I stayed together, angry sad people, to continue a normal life for the children. We tried to gut it out. I thought about the early days of our marriage, when we played and worked together, raised three babies who were in no doubt of our love. Would things have been different if I had told Winkie about the Church's goal for me, told her before we married? Maybe she'd have stood by me to accept the situation, trying to believe I could change. It's possible she could have avoided such a sense of humiliation if George hadn't come out of nowhere to her. I will never know ... I never gave her that chance. I will regret how I hurt her forever.

While the Church was willing to turn its back on me, Bishop Gregory wasn't. He found a program they would accept called Gay Aversion Therapy. It was my last chance to be cured. I knew it would fail, but Bishop Gregory believed in it. Winkie demanded that I enroll.

The program cost me what little was left of my self-respect and pride. It was painful mentally and physically. I cringe just thinking about it. My penis was hooked to an electrical device, then I was given a book of pictures, mostly photos of beautiful scenery. When a photo of a nude man appeared, I was given a shock. The humiliation was overwhelming, as I docilely accepted this painful therapy invented for sex offenders and deviants.

I took it for three weeks before I broke. As the therapist approached me with his wires, I screamed that I couldn't wait for the shock so I could see the nude man. "Bring it on," I growled at him. That ended the shock treatments, but therapy continued for two years.

Nobody can say I didn't try. I didn't want to lose my Church, but I finally was beaten. The Church could do nothing for me. God and I were on our own with each other.

My therapist's only answer for his failure was, "Sometimes you have to pretend to be something you're not, in order to become what you want to be."

I was enraged. "Fuck you!" I cried. "That's what I've been doing all my life, and I'm still not straight."

Bishop Gregory finally understood. He wept, acknowledging that homosexuality was nothing to be cured.

"Tell others," I said.

"I cannot," he answered.

He would have been fired, excommunicated, shunned. His was the only apology I ever received, in secret and unofficial.

A heart attack soon followed the therapy sessions. Winkie did not come to see me in the three days I was in intensive care. She did contact my mother and explain the situation. You'll remember my mother ... she's been out of the story a while. We had nothing to say to each other. But she called now. When I picked up the phone she screamed, "That bitch wife of yours told me you were a faggot." She rattled off such awful names, I've never heard the like before or since. Then she hung up on me. Even my mother the whore found me too low to stay in her life.

After three years of trying, Winkie and I gave it up. She'd been as taken in by the Mormons as I was. If they'd done what they said they could, her marriage would still be sound. The Church was my partner in the agony we put her through, but her fury was with me, not them.

My wife, the lovable, fun Winkie, was destroyed. "I'll never be able to trust my own opinion again," she said. She never smiled anymore. I was to blame. Winkie couldn't stand what I had done, nor was she interested in trying to understand. It was past time for me to go.

I rented an apartment close by; friends from work helped me move. When they left, I fell to the floor in that solitary place and wept for the misery a mistaken belief, lies, and cheating can cause. I grieved.

But at last the time had come for me to start over with a life that was honest. It was time to live openly as a gay man.

12.

Coming Out

After the noise level of my former busy household, the apartment was as silent as the proverbial tomb. It was a great place to have a giant sulk.

As a little boy, I was so bereft of parental affection that I could have easily assumed I wasn't worth a damn. But I had an older sister going through many of the same things I was handling, so I knew I wasn't the cause of our problems. Jacquie always tried to protect us both. And I had a supportive teacher who recognized my art talent; I was convinced I would be something. So even in the worst of times, I remained afloat. I was an inexplicably positive kid who believed good things awaited.

That outlook saved me now, helping me climb out of the lowest level of hell. Self-flagellation or suicide were no answers; my own children were having a tough time as it was. I needed to man up for them and be sure none of them felt the break-up was their fault.

I did not intend to abandon my kids. They needed their dad to be a constant. The boys were livid with me for hurting their mother; they egged each other on with that fury. As only young teens can, they set many high hurdles for me to win them back. During our first visits after the separation, they moped. My daughter Laura was another issue. She wanted me at home so much that her mother and she began to grate on each other.

All three had to be convinced I was there for the long haul, that whatever was between their mother and me was not their fault. Being responsible for your children's sense of wellbeing will snap you out of your own wound-licking faster than anything else.

Winkie's anger at me often hurt them, crossing the border into vindictive territory. She played games like not telling the kids I called, or deleting my messages, or making sure they had no clean clothes when I picked them up. Winkie also stopped cleaning the house, knowing I'd do it when she was gone. I would never let my kids live in a barnyard, and she called my bluff.

One day, Jeff sniped at me because I didn't go see his twin, Doug, when he was in the hospital. He had been hit by a car, and Winkie never told me. My understanding of her rage began to tarnish after the first months. Her bitter behavior allowed me to stop feeling like the only guilty party. One day I stomped into the bank where she worked and announced to one and all what stunts she was pulling. That was the first day I actually felt I might survive our break-up.

After that we rarely saw each other when I picked up the kids for a movie or weekend camping trips to the mountains or the beach. Apparently our old setter Kelly missed me. One day when Laura buried me in sand on the beach, Kelly laid down next to my head to lick my cheek and forehead.

While saving my relationship with my children, I was also battling with my relationship with God. My Mormon "friends" sided with Winkie so I felt the coldness of their disapproval. My work place was my escape, the only place I heard much chatter or laughter. I don't know if God was angry with me, but I was certainly angry with Him.

As far as committing to live an honest life as a gay man, I had to figure out what that even meant. It had been thirty years since I lived with James; back then, homosexuality was hounded by the law. There was no public display of affection between men. Now, gays were freer than before. In fact, it was very easy to be promiscuous in the late-seventies, early-eighties. Gay parades had begun in major cities; sodomy laws were collapsing. The "handkerchief code" bespoke preferences, demands for civil rights increased in volume, students and politicians were coming out. Fear was still there, but it was pushed to the back seat as men who'd lived in secrecy were able to breathe free. I had been an observer of this change during my marriage, and now I was a participant. I, as a forty-something, was free to act like a horny twenty-something in terms of sampling the great buffet around me.

Being free to sample didn't mean I'd actually do it. The disgust of the Church followed me around like a personal thunder cloud. And what would my kids think? Consequently, I didn't dive into the deep end right off the bat.

There was a gay bar not far from my office. I'd heard rumors about the Skylark as long as I worked in San Bernardino. As I became convinced I should get a toe wet in my new society, I began to drive past the Skylark. Again and again. Slowing down a time or two. Building up my nerve to actually park in their lot.

I tried for nonchalance. That might have been easier if I had been a drinker; I'd never had beer or a mixed drink, nothing alcoholic other than the French wines (Mormon, you know). I knew little about bars at all, much less gay bars. Maybe it would be easier to sidle in the back door. That's what I decided to do.

I opened the door and noticed an oval-shaped bar before the door closed behind me. Then I went blind, California afternoon sun overshadowed by bar murk.

Are there no lights at all? Is that how people keep from being recognized?

I stood paralyzed in the dark. With enough squinting, I eventually picked out the bar again and fumbled my way over to it. I had no idea what drink to order so I requested a Coke.

As my eyes adjusted, I was amazed to see women. I had assumed it would only be men. Then someone put a hand on my shoulder and asked, "Wayne! What are you doing here?"

I yelped, my blood pressure shooting to the sky. It was one of my employees.

Oh God, oh no!

I managed, "Ah, um ... thought I'd have a drink before going home. Set it up, barkeep."

Barkeep looked at me like I was an idiot. "Another Coke coming up," he said.

My employee leaned in to whisper, "Did you know this is a gay bar?"

"No!" I faked dumbfounded. "Really? Why are you here?"

"I came to shoot pool. Join us if you want." He and his buddies headed for the tables.

I was stunned. I looked at my close friend Barkeep and asked, "Is that true? Is he gay? Are these others gay? The women, too?"

Barkeep smiled at the newbie. "Is the Pope Catholic?"

The Skylark became a home away from home, filled with people pretty much like me. It was a thrill that nearly overwhelmed this middle-aged man.

Imagine! Free to approach another man. Astounding!

I got into the swing of things pretty darn quick. Men actually asked me out. And in time, I worked up the confidence to ask some of them out. Dinner dates and movie dates frequently ended in my apartment or his. The strangest occurrence happened one early morning when my bedmate received a call from a furious Cher; our dalliance had screwed up her hair appointment with him.

I had my share of raunchy couplings in dark corners and seedy backrooms, as well as trysts in elegant hotels. In for a penny, in for a pound. This was the most promiscuous period of my life, and I reveled in it. It was exciting to head out after work, not knowing what might happen before morning.

A couple years passed this way. I was greatly complimented to be desirable after I'd felt so bad about myself. Rarely was I rejected by someone who intrigued me. However, this lifestyle finally lost its glitter. I craved a long-term partner. It's what I had always wanted; sex for its own sake did not pleasure me for long. I needed a lasting relationship, like the one with James could have been, should have been.

The Skylark was my main hang-out; it replaced the Mormon Church for fellowship, not that either establishment would like that comparison. I met men in situations similar to mine, men who had been married but were now exploring the life they'd wanted to begin with. I also grew close to two lesbians, Judy and Sandy, who were more fun than anyone I'd ever known.

Judy talked me into joining her gay bowling league. One evening we were walking out of the alley, my arm around Judy, just as Winkie and friends in her league were coming in. My ex froze and stared, then asked, "Who is this woman?"

"This is my new girlfriend," I answered, then Judy and I walked away. I'm ashamed to admit I was tickled to give Winkie something to wonder about.

One Friday after work I was with Judy and a couple friends at the Skylark when a rowdy group of young men were having a party around the pool table. It was a twenty-first birthday for their friend named Joe. He was flying high, and when I wished him a happy birthday, he grabbed me and gave me a juicy smacker right on the lips.

Well now, well now.

I saw him again at a gay disco I attended with Judy and Sandy. He was far too young for me but, oh, so good looking. Judy whispered to me, "Quit hanging with the women folk, asshole. Get over there and do what you want to do."

She's always been a sweet talker.

Joe and I danced, talked, laughed, and danced some more. I flung my arms around like John Travolta, acting the fool in my joy. I suppose I'm lucky that my neck didn't balloon out like a hooded seal or my butt turn bright red like a baboon. Human mating rituals are a bit more restrained than that, but not by much.

I asked Joe to lunch. That lunch was followed by a dinner later in the week. And another.

It was complicated. Joe lived with his alcoholic parents and worked with his sister at a hair salon they shared. He was not ready to come out. Of course, his sister Danielle knew. She was cold to me, thinking I was too old for Joe. I know this because she said to me, "You're too old for Joe."

Frankly, I agreed; ours was a twenty-year age difference. Was I playing the part of James, assigning my original role as boy-man to Joe? Was I enjoying introducing a male ingénue from a bad family to better things in life? And so what if I was? Joe said he didn't care about the age gap, so I quit worrying, too.

After dating for a month, we spent our first night together. It was special, I think because Joe was eager but not as experienced as an old timer like me. If anyone was the aggressor, it was me. He moved into my apartment soon after that, and we taught each other how to be the perfect lovers for each other. I don't remember ever discussing whether to have a committed relationship; it simply was one from the beginning. Gay marriage was not legal, but we didn't need it to be.

In the early going, my good-natured lover surprised me with his nightmares, savage ones that awakened him in tears and night sweats. I held him tight as, over time, he revealed the phantoms of his past. His father had abused both his mother and Joe. It went on until Daddy Dearest burned every shred of her clothes on the lawn, then attacked her with a butcher knife. Joe got between them, ending up in the hospital, bloodied by the knife. Both parents blamed him, two pathetic drunks dependent on each other. Joe escaped them when he moved in with me; he finally understood that there was nothing he could do for them. I knew he had ghosts to bury, just as I had dealt with mine. It might take years, but I had the time. After a year, he stopped having the nightmares.

We found it fun to share our interests. I took him to art galleries, and he took me to monster truck rallies (I hated them). I took him to all the Southern Cal beaches, and he took me to an ELO concert. It was even more fun to experience new things together. We'd never been to plays or musicals so we saw *Sleuth* and *Man From La Mancha*. We took the bus tour of celebrity houses while visiting Los Angeles, and lost repeatedly at Santa Anita betting on horses by color. In San Bernardino, we toured every museum, from railroad memorabilia to the original McDonald's site. Judy and I taught him how to bowl, and he taught me tennis.

James and I had never been able to do such things together out in the open; we were still in the grips of a hostile world. Being in public with my lover added a whole new dimension of delight to the world of this gay man.

We bought a house with four bedrooms to be big enough for my kids if they chose to visit. Laura moved in. She was done with her mother and vice versa; Winkie told her that she reminded her too much of me. My sons chose to stay with their mother, but we kept up visits and outings with each other.

Laura lived with me for many years, until she married and moved away. She liked Joe. They clowned with each other, often forming a bond against me when it came to what movie to see or whether pizza or Thai sounded best. Before she moved in, I had told her we needed to talk.

"Are you going to tell me you're gay?" she asked.

I looked at her in surprise; it was nothing Winkie or I had told her. "How do you know that?"

"Your apartment had one bedroom."

Smart kid. "Do your brothers know?"

She shrugged. "I don't know. They're stupid."

One day the boys came over to have a swim in our pool followed by dinner. It became a frequent occurrence. I decided it was time to have "The Talk" with them as I had their little sister.

I hemmed, hawed, and spit it out. "I'm gay, and Joe is my lover."

Doug nodded.

Jeff said, "Sure, Dad. Can we watch TV?"

I had a family again. My job was going well. The social life I lost along with the Church had come back to me, in a very different set of friends that accepted me for what I was. I believed in God the Almighty and his Son our Savior; I just didn't believe in the Mormons as gatekeepers anymore. I would find something better. For now, life flourished.

I had two remaining slaps from the Church as a going away present. A girl told the Bishop that Laura was having sex with all kinds of boys. It was not true, but the Bishop took her into his office and accused her of sleeping around. She was very hurt. When she moved in with Joe and me, she never went to that Church again. And when my sons proudly accepted their final Eagle Scout awards, a member of my old congregation stood to say it was remarkable that they had succeeded with such a deviant for a father. I left, not wanting to embarrass my boys any more than that bastard had already done.

Joe was a wonderful gardener. He landscaped our yard with the creativity he applied to a haircut ... it was manicured at all times. While I was at work, he installed a fifty-five gallon fish tank that required four delivery men to lug it in. Joe and I went to the pet store again and again for the right pump, heater, gravel, decorations. In a week, it was set and the temperature was perfect. We proudly brought home a stunning array of tropical fish. It was beautiful, and it enthralled us to sit and watch in the evening. More than us, it entranced our Doberman, Tuffy. He could have taken down a street gang all on his own, but he was terrified of a clown fish.

I was the chef since Joe cooked nothing but frozen pizza. But he did the cleaning. Our joy attracted others to our home, so our pool parties became legendary. We danced at the gay disco, loved seeing movies, and read aloud to each other, passages from whatever books were intriguing us at the time.

Joe and I both liked to camp so it was a big part of our vacations together. Our farthest journey was to Banff and Lake Louise in Canada, loving that beautiful environment, the hikes, and even the ranger talks. We couldn't fit much more than a two-man tent and a Coleman lantern into my MG, but we made do. Often we drove the Rim of the World Highway from San Bernardino through Big Bear to where our friends Judy and Sandy had a cabin. All four of us relished the outdoor ice rink where we rented skates and proceeded to gather black and blue spots on our butts, counting them like notches on a gun.

Joe and I wanted to see the world. I certainly was eager to visit Paris and New York again. He desired a Caribbean cruise, although the west coast of Mexico would have been much closer. After the cruises I'd taken to and from Paris many years earlier, I wasn't all that keen. Instead, we booked a trip to Hawaii. It sounded exotic as we worked with a travel agent (one we knew from the Skylark). He helped us with our flight and places to stay, plus a boat tour around the islands, a bus tour of Oahu, and two days in Kauai. It was a couple months out, so our excitement had time to grow. Neither of us had flown before or worn leis and paddled outriggers or had sex on the beach.

It was 1983, and we were one. Joe received a powerful new management job at a national hair salon, bought his first new car, and retired the junker that had become as unreliable as the future. He was driving home from the salon one night when a drunk driver ran a stop sign, careening into his new car on the driver side.

My love was killed instantly.

My name was on a card in Joe's wallet to notify in case of emergency. I identified his broken body at the site of the crash. Shock set it, and my daughter Laura helped me navigate those first days. At the funeral, friends from the salon, the disco, my office, the Skylark, and elsewhere mourned with me. I gave Joe's parents the things they claimed were his, and I told them to never come back.

A month later I took our trip to Hawaii on my own. Joe was supposed to be there with me, laughing and exclaiming at everything new. I looked for his spirit everywhere, on my own in that beautiful paradise. I would never return to those islands, I knew that even then.

I'd faced enough sorrow in my life to be good at it. In days gone by, I'd managed to keep a beacon of hope on the horizon. But after Joe died, I fell apart.

13.

Starting Over. Again.

I've been trying to figure a way to write this chapter without statements like, "When the lifeblood drained out of Joe, it drained out of me as well," or "I cried until there were no tears left." You've no doubt suffered loss yourself; you know the power and shock of grief. I couldn't stand to be alone; I couldn't stand not to be alone. I wanted to remember Joe; I wanted to forget him. I was exhausted; I couldn't sleep.

My strong work ethic helped in those early months post-Joe, just as it had when Winkie and I split up. My personal life was never a deterrent to the performance I could deliver; I carried on like a champ for GE. In the next few years, the company moved me from San Bernardino to Anaheim and Santa Clara, always to help an office increase its productivity.

A side note: I'd enjoyed my two decades with GE. But new management challenged my sense of fair play in 1989. Changes in employee benefits were being made that hurt the people reporting to me, and that distressed me to no end. I complained enough to be shown the door.

But I'm getting ahead of my story. I owe so much to my daughter Laura and my friend Judy for helping me through Joe's death. These two women soothed my aches as much as anyone could. Laura made sure I took long walks whenever I needed, which was often. She held my hand as we went, both of us soothed by each other's company. Joe had been her friend, too. Judy sat with me in her home for long hours to pass the time after work, until I thought I could go home and rest.

Women are better with emotions than men are. They are allowed to have them, show them, express them even when they aren't drinking. Laura and Judy could tolerate being around a man who might burst into earsplitting howls at any second. Laura continued to live with her dear old dad; Judy continued to offer me her cabin as a retreat.

Judy had a military lover at this time, a domineering woman tough as nails. One night when I arrived, Soldier Girl was beating the crap out of Judy. In a rage, she turned her well-trained violence onto me with a powerhouse punch. I hit her back. I can't say I'm proud to have decked a woman, but I never saw one be so violent. Judy continued to be my friend, but Soldier Girl disappeared from both of our lives that very day.

The late eighties are mostly a blur for me. Without Joe, I was not interested in another lover. I did frequent a gay coffee house in Santa Clara to make friends, after Laura and I moved to that area. At the urging of this new group, I went to a New Year's Eve party at a gay bar. Another life lesson learned: if you are grieving, stay away from places where people are rejoicing. I pretended to be happy, a part of the jolly crowd. But I was dying inside. Basically a teetotaler, I nonetheless got raging drunk that night. I was so smashed, I had to search for my car. When I finally found it, I couldn't see straight to drive home. The world spun until I conked out and slept in the car until the middle of New Year's Day.

My days were easier if I observed them from afar, as if somebody else was going through them:

First the sad man gets up and showers, then he goes to the office to pretend to give a damn, then he watches a double feature until he can meander home in misery for another empty night.

This spacing out, a form of dissociation from the world around me, went on for months. At the same time, the hysteria over AIDS was taking off like a rocket. It was at the front of everyone's mind, nowhere more so than among gay men. As if my personal tragedy wasn't enough, the eradication of us all was the thought for the day.

We didn't know what was safe and what wasn't, a kiss or a hand to hold or a dentist appointment. For many of us, all sexual contact stopped, unprotected or otherwise. Joe and I had been a committed couple, so I'd felt safe enough then. The height of the AIDS scare dovetailed with my lack of interest in other partners. Concern for myself was not as great as concern for my friends; it appeared there were people with HIV who were willfully passing it on to innocent partners. I couldn't imagine such cruelty.

Unbeknownst to GE, they were instrumental in kick-starting me back into life. The company flew me to New York for a meeting of office managers. I had so much vacation time backed up, HR highly suggested I use it or lose it, so I added a week to my trip.

From the instant I got out of a cab at our Manhattan meeting facility, New York swept me up, just as it had in years past. The city decidedly has a siren song with such lyrics as "you haven't lived until you've lived here," and "sample my riches and you'll never be the same," and "I can spit you out any time I wish." Loving New York is like loving a dragon.

After the managers meeting, I moved to the YMCA for my vacation time. Who could afford NY hotels even in the 80s? I was astounded when I went to clean up. The shower room writhed like a ball of baby snakes, but these were nude men performing the most personal of acts in the most public of manners. I dashed out of there, knowing if AIDS was anywhere, it was in the YMCA shower room.

I walked the streets during the days, visiting museums and galleries, fine restaurants and corner delis. The city's splendor revived me, as though it were a Salvation Show. I visited the gay part of the city, a mecca for men my age with more in mind than behaving like beasts in showers and bath houses. Christopher Street, in the west portion of Manhattan's Greenwich Village, is home to the Stonewall Inn where the original gay riots of June 1969 began, opposing police violence against our kind. It is the traditional start of gay liberation in the United States, when gays and lesbians of New York came together as a powerful new community to protest gender obstacles. The first gay parade marches began a year later; Joe and I had participated in one in Los Angeles. The Gay Pride movement grew across the country and the world.

As I walked, I saw a good-looking couple who also seemed to be touring the area. One said hello, so the three of us went on together. Terrance was an artist who'd recently moved back to the city and was showing his visiting friend around. We went to a tiny art gallery, where Terrance exhibited his paintings, each a wild slash of color very unlike my own impressionism. It was his turn to mind the store for all the artists who exhibited there.

Terrance was thrilled I was from Venice Beach because he was, too. As I began to question him, he began to backtrack. He wasn't exactly from there but had recently stayed there with friends. I gave him my phone number because he asked, and that was that. When the week ended, I flew back to California, somewhat revived by my vacation. I didn't think about Terrance again, not for months, until he called to say he was coming to stay with his friends in Venice Beach again. He wanted me to visit.

I'd been with nobody since Joe. Was it time for me to stumble forward? I could at least meet up with Terrance, see if it felt right. I went for the weekend. We walked the boardwalk, chatting openly. I remembered how secretive everything had to be with James many years before, in this very spot. Now we did not fear arrest. The memory fanned the little flame that burned for my first love. What had become of him?

Terrance's friends were a lesbian couple, Glenda and Sarah. They were a delight, being a couple of tough, smart, cynical New Yorkers. I found myself laughing and enjoying the day more freely than I had in ages. But when we returned to their apartment, Glenda took me aside while Terrance and Sarah were concocting cocktails in the kitchen. She told me to be careful, that Terrance had AIDS. I was confounded by, and furious with, Terrance. How could he? How dare he? My first interest since Joe, and this happened. I packed up and drove home, full of rage and self-pity.

It was Glenda who eventually dug my head out of my rump for me. "Terrance's plight is far greater than yours," she said on the phone the next day. "Give him a break." She was right. I saw it more clearly once the immediate heat dissipated. Terrance had not asked me to have sex ... I had assumed it was his goal. I could have the decency to allow room for friendship. Terrance and I did keep in touch until he died a few months later. Glenda and I became fast friends and remain so today. If I ever marry another woman, Glenda will be my first choice. Wow, how the Church finger-pointers would squeal about that!

Joe's death, followed by Terrance's, started a sequence of funerals in my extended family. Jacquie's father David, the man who never claimed me, died in 1987 in St. George, Utah. Jacquie was still in Mexico and did not attend his service. I understand his current wife and children were there.

His death closed a door for me. I would never discover who my real father was. I doubt my mother even knew, a downside of her profession. And there was simply nobody else to ask. It is an unsolved mystery.

Speaking of my mother, she had long since married a Mormon named Paul. They lived in a nice little house in Venice Beach. Paul died of a heart attack just months after Jacquie's father. So to Venice Beach I went. That funky little town kept calling me back like a boomerang. I began to feel I'd never escape.

My mother and I didn't exactly have a bad relationship; we had no relationship. We'd given up on each other many years earlier. If I had felt there was anyone else to help with the funeral, I wouldn't have bothered going. But I had no quarrel with Paul, and the job needed to be done.

When I went into their house, I discovered that Mama was now wheelchair-bound. A member of the Mormon Church was helping her. My mother greeted me with, "Well, Queer, why are you here?" Ah, family reunions.

I steered clear of her as much as possible as I paid the funeral expenses and bought a double-depth grave site for Paul now and my mother when her time came. I figured he was the only one who would want her near, even in death. After the funeral, I found a caregiver for Mama, then I got out of Dodge.

Of course, that wasn't the end of it. A couple months later, the caregiver called to let me know Mama was getting a second trust deed on her house in order to buy a trailer.

"Really?" I sputtered. As far as I knew, my mother would have no idea how to negotiate such a thing. Other than her clear understanding that I was a faggot, her mind was definitely slipping. Maybe the reason was early onset dementia, or maybe poor lifestyle choices made as a young prostitute. "Who's helping her with that?"

"His name is Dick," said the caregiver.

Dick! You'll remember Dick, my sister's first husband. The one I was supposed to kill if he didn't leave Mexico. The one who wanted his baby back but apparently changed his mind because he never made another attempt at it. Yep. That Dick. What on earth was he doing meddling with my mother's finances?

He'd talked the miserable old crone out of her house and into a trailer on his property. He arranged for a second trust deed on her house, and took the money from it. I told him I would press charges if he didn't return the money. He must have been pretty scared of me ... maybe he thought I was still out to kill him. At least he did as requested. I sold the house and moved Mama to another home in San Jose, not far from where I lived with Laura. I hired a young woman to cook and clean for my mother even though she never forgave me for moving her away from that nice man, Dick. Laura and I were her primary ties to life, and she hated us both for it.

In time, I had to face a tough decision about my mother. She really couldn't live alone. Laura was newly married and largely pregnant, but she agreed that her miserable old grandmother was a liability to herself. I finally introduced my mother to a very nice nursing home.

She went completely berserk. The language she used to the admissions people was worse than any she'd used on me, and that was legendary. The admissions people blanched, looked wide-eyed at me, told me to leave and take that nasty old piece of work with me. I assumed that word would spread to every tolerable place to beware.

It was almost funny. I'd spent so many years being unacceptable to her, now she was unacceptable to polite society. No Mormons stepped up to help. I could either kick her to the curb in her wheelchair, or move her into the home I shared with my daughter and her husband.

I took the upper story, and the rest of the pack were on the very spacious ground floor. It was a nightmare from the beginning. One day, a very-round Laura was attaching a lunch tray to the wheelchair when her grandmother reached up, grabbed her long red hair, pulled her close, and hit my daughter in the abdomen. Did Mama realize Laura was pregnant? Was she trying to kill the baby? Did she care?

I lost all composure. I knew that Mama had been a cheerless wretch for a very long time. Maybe she was in her right mind, maybe not. But I flew into her room, grabbed the wheelchair by the arms, and shook it like a pit bull with a ragdoll. "If you EVER hurt Laura again, it's the old folks home for you. And any facility that will take you will be a ghastly place to live."

That's about the last conversation I ever had with her, and I guess you can't really call that a conversation. She died not many months later. I had her body shipped to Venice Beach for burial in the plot above Paul. My sister Jacquie joined me graveside, but neither of us shed a tear. We even laughed that, once again, Mama was on top.

Any mourning involving our mother had been done many years before.

Joe was gone, Mama was dead, GE was out of my life, my kids were doing well. Laura's baby was fine, in fact is a joy to me as my oldest grandchild. It was time I picked up a telescope and aimed at my future. What would I do, as a middle-aged beginner? I didn't want to work for another company. I wanted to run my own.

GE had sent me on my way with a stack of benefits, and I'd sold the house that I'd bought for my mother. For the first time in my life, I had enough cash to consider a business of my own. I knew I couldn't make a living from my art, and while I had done well as a paperboy, I was looking for something a bit more grandiose. But what? I considered my own history. What job had I enjoyed the most?

It didn't take long for me to move the concession stand to the top of the list. I liked doing business with real consumers instead of electrical contractors. I liked food service. As crazy as it could get, it had been a blast, and a big dollop of fun was just the ticket.

But this time, I'd do it on a grander scale. Something more permanent than a food truck. Maybe a restaurant. Or, better yet, a coffee shop. It was the late-eighties, so the market wasn't flooded with designer coffees. I didn't want the hassle of a liquor license, but the idea of coffee tickled me to no end. A good Mormon should never enjoy a cup. But an excommunicated

Mormon would not only enjoy it, but sell it to others. I'd be a caffeine lord, aiding and abetting buzzed moods and sleepless nights city wide. Oh, my wicked, wicked ways!

I talked with Laura about it, and she thought it would be a fun thing to do; she agreed to be my co-manager. I began to look for space in downtown Santa Cruz and followed ads in *Nation's Restaurant News* in case an existing shop might come up for sale. Nothing did.

But a retail space in the old Cooper House won my heart. This was the center of things "cool" where trendsetters hung out in Santa Cruz. Anybody who was anybody gathered here to chat and people-watch.

I called it Wayne's Brews & Bakes. Laura and I sold all kinds of coffees and espresso as well as sweet rolls, Noah's bagels, and ice cream. At lunch we offered knuckle-buster sandwiches on baguettes from a local bakery. On our outdoor patio, you could hear the music and laughter from the bar next door, so it always felt festive. Within a few months, Laura and I had four other employees.

I loved it. We were crazy busy with both gay and straight customers. I began looking at the local scenery, feeling ready for another relationship that lasted longer than a large drip coffee. Since I was a business owner I didn't allow myself to go too wild, but there was one sight I wanted to see: the nude beach on the edge of town. I finally went, although I kept my suit on.

The gays there that day didn't attract me, but a handsome young man with a beautiful young woman certainly did. I ambled close enough to stare. Unfortunately, he thought I was staring at her and told me to piss off.

Soon thereafter, I met the perfect person for this stage of my life. Jim was my age and more interested in a friend than a lover. He'd had his share of hotties, and now the idea of AIDS terrified him. Also, he had a crackpot aunt who told him he'd go to hell for bedding other men. He semi-believed her.

"Is she a Mormon?" I asked, surprised that she wasn't.

I was the better for his company in many ways. He was a program designer who helped me update Wayne's Brews. No more hand inventories or cash register shenanigans. We visited a gay resort he knew on the Russian River, and the next day he taught me how to fly a glider released from a tow plane. The peace and beauty of that flight is as close to a miracle as I'll ever get.

If you like a happy ending, this nearly was it.

But in 1989, Mother Nature stepped in. The Loma Prieta Earthquake destroyed the Cooper House. As the old walls began to shiver, I raced through the building to be sure everyone was out. Then I ran back to my shop to get the cash box, but the fire department wouldn't allow me back in. People in the building next door were dying. I stood in shock, not knowing what to do. Wayne's

Brews was not insured because the old building didn't meet earthquake standards.

I went to my car and sat. I already knew my shop was a total loss. I'd invested every nickel into that beloved enterprise.

At last, I drove home. A broken beam had crashed through our dining room. As I gathered tools from a storage shed to support what I could, a strong aftershock ripped through the area. The whole upper story collapsed into the downstairs, and the exterior walls fell outward.

My business was demolished; my home was gone. I can read symbolism as well as the next guy; this was the end of my life in Santa Cruz. Laura, her husband, and baby moved elsewhere in San Jose. I headed to San Francisco, alone once more.

14.

San Francisco

Venice Beach ... Paris ... Lee Vining ... Santa Monica ... San Bernardino ... Santa Cruz ... San Francisco. How many times in my life would I have to start over? Was I to blame, or was I an unwilling victim of circumstance? Disruptive change was a constant element in my life. Sorrow never stayed away long whether I invited it in unwillingly, or it snuck in, stealthy as a cat.

Long before the 1990s, San Francisco drew gays like a super magnet. I was a little late to the party. I was also old enough to beware the sex available on every corner; age and AIDS were powerful deterrents to unzipping just anywhere.

Not that I was without desire. I still hoped for a relationship. Like Weebles, I wobbled, but I didn't fall down.

I was jobless and not inclined to spend much on my digs, so I came up with the first and last months' rent on a studio apartment not far from the Oakland Bay Bridge. I decorated with a new futon and television. In order to eat at the counter in my miniscule kitchen, I bought a stool. Two of them, actually, in case I ever had a guest. All that I salvaged from the wreckage of my Santa Cruz home was about half a wardrobe.

Westinghouse employed me once again, but my manager hated "fags." I reminded him that San Francisco had discrimination laws, but that didn't curb his tongue. Finally my co-workers complained about how he treated me, and he was gone the following week. Jugheads like him would do better to live anywhere else in the nation.

As I grew comfortable in the city, I moved to a one-bedroom in Twin Peaks that had a great view. Remember Jim, the celibate man I met in Santa Cruz? He surprised the hell out of me by purchasing a dining table and chairs for me; his current beau called me a time or two, to say he couldn't figure Jim out. What I knew about him, I kept to myself. Jim remains one of the few people I have known who wanted a great deal less than he willingly gave.

As I grew comfortable in the city, I went to the Castro district for lunches and friendships. It was (still is) a beautiful community of little shops, open patios, refined lifestyles. It was a safe haven for middle-income gays and lesbians. I remember reading an article that called it the Gay Utopia, and in many ways it was. Even the cops who served the area were often gay so in case of crime, we could count on immediate response.

But I had a darker side, too. I liked a good bad-boy party. For that I went to the bars in the South of Market Area (SOMA). SOMA was industrial and red neck; how the hell it attracted leather bars, bear bars, and S&M bars I will never know. Neighbors down there threatened us nightly, and we threatened back. On Sunday mornings, I frequented an S&M joint that served all the beer you could drink for two bucks. Now you know I was no drinker, so I wasn't there for the brewski. In fact, one glass lasted me the day.

For evening entertainment, I checked out the leather bars. The outfits hooked me, and I developed a new sense of fashion that included black leather and chains. I might not mention this part of my nature, but it is important in what happened next. You can't wear leathers unless you have a bike, right? What else could I do but purchase a Honda Gold Wing from another denizen of the leather crowd? It was flashy red, shiny chrome, and hotter than a steak on a grill.

I took the safety classes then hit the road. It was wonderful, reminding me of the freedom of gliding but with more noise. The hills, the twisting streets, braiding through traffic, wind in my hair and beard, no helmet required. I was hot shit, brother.

At least I was until a woman coming up the hill toward Twin Peaks, in a vehicle the size and shape of a Sherman tank, slammed into me. She blasted me across two lanes of traffic and onto a curb. Since she had run a red light in order to accomplish this feat, I had plenty of witnesses come running. I remember thinking I should get up and get their names. But I couldn't get up. My body refused to act on my brain's commands.

An ambulance took me to UCSF where they discovered my right arm and leg were dislocated. They put me back together like a string of pop beads, loaded me up with pain killers, and sent me on my way. My friend Jim drove me home where I spent ten days trying to recover.

The woman's insurance company offered to settle for $15,000. After I involved a lawyer, we settled for $60,000, which paid for the bike (total wreck) and the lawyer. My insurance through Westinghouse covered the medical bills and physical therapy. I ended up with $40,000 and no vehicle. My biker days were done.

But that didn't mean my days in SOMA were done. I had discovered a great affection for bear bars. The most famous one is the Lone Star Saloon. It was there back then; it's still there today. The owners and patrons have nicknamed the place Bear Bar USA.

For you uninitiated, when a gay man says bear, he means a big hairy dude. A furry, muscular man is what he seeks and what he's likely to be himself. I had a beard, ample hair on my chest, and elsewhere. I worked out many days a week in a gay gym to stay in shape. Jeans-and-flannel was the usual lumberjack-ish wardrobe back then, and the leather bars were open to bears and vice versa.

With my hirsute body, ample size and height, I fit right into this crowd. In fact, on one of my initial visits to scope it out, there was a contest for newcomers. Someone nominated me, and I became Trophy Bear for the month. Ha! After that, I joined the club. And that's how I heard of Shanti.

The Lone Star sponsored many events for bears. One evening, representatives of the Shanti Project spoke to us. Shanti is Sanskrit for inner peace. Their group goals include peer support and guidance for those with life-threatening conditions, particularly AIDS sufferers in those days. The group still exists, and a quick internet search can provide you with all the details you might want.

I became a volunteer. I was given two clients, each as similar to me as possible. Shanti wanted a volunteer to have as much empathy as he could. Both men had been married and raised families. One owned a home on the city's west side, and the other was in a Castro apartment over a hardware store. Their names were Sam and Lewis. Both were dying.

My job was to make their lives easier. I helped them with their wills and final directives, then called in a Shanti lawyer to be sure everything was legal. I worked with Sam and Lewis to develop lists of whom I should notify when they went to the hospital and when they died. I helped them pay their bills (often covering them myself), shopped for groceries, picked up cleaning, walked dogs, whatever they needed. We talked about our families, how they had or hadn't accepted us as gay, what things we most feared. We told jokes and belly laughed, shared dinners and watched movies. Lewis, a flirt who never gave up trying to lure me in, was also a gorgeous woman when he was in drag. "Lulu" surprised me on the street once in full regalia; I didn't recognize him until he hit on me! I spent several hours a week with each of them and met with other Shanti volunteers so we could share ideas.

Sam and Lewis died within a week of each other, nearly two years after we met. I grieved for both of these charmers when their lights went out. AIDS was a fact of life for the people who I considered my peers. As months passed, medical science rushed along ahead of many of us. We got smarter about what we could do physically and what we couldn't (this was true for straights as well, once it was admitted that AIDS wasn't a disease just for homosexuals).

I began to date, carefully. A clinic in Castro gave us blood tests whenever we wanted, so I knew I was clean of infection. This was a period in my life when I met many terrific men, but found I could not stand deception of any kind. The second I became aware a potential partner had other men on his string, I was done with him.

One weekend in the Castro, I was having breakfast, watching all the boys walk by. Through the restaurant window, I saw Glenda and Sarah stroll past, arm in arm. These were the lesbians from Venice Beach who were Terrance's friends. I ran out calling to them, then dragged them back in to have breakfast with me. They'd moved to Oakland. We started a tradition of going out to breakfast on weekends. These two were my best friends in San Francisco for most of the time I lived there. They accompanied me to Beer Busts at the Lone Star, tried to set me up, supported me when another potential soul mate showed his true colors. As matchmakers they were failures, but I loved them for trying.

While my romances dwindled, I was getting rich. It surprised me as much as anybody else. I took the insurance settlement money and got back into the coffee business, along with my friend Jim.

We purchased a coffee cart. He lasted in the business about a week once he saw how much work it was, so I was on my own. I called the cart Wayne's Brews, of course, as a doff of my hat to my shop in Santa Cruz. My cart location was in an office complex at the corner of Francisco and Montgomery streets, where it provided the area's first designer coffee drinks. I was only open weekdays, 6 a.m. to 3 p.m. so was flabbergasted by the instant popularity of Wayne's Brews.

I worked by myself for a week. Business grew. And grew. I hired a young woman to help. Then a young man. Pat, Mike, and I toiled happily together, a fun team to be around with cups of morning magic for office workers. The business grew some more.

By the end of the first month, I gave Pat and Mike raises. The head of the FBI in Northern California was my first customer every day. Barbara Boxer and Dianne Feinstein put a stop at Wayne's Brews on their busy schedules.

I opened a second cart just six blocks away from the first and made Pat the manager of one, Mike the manager of the other. I could walk back and forth keeping them both supplied and taking money to the bank. We hired two more people, and I set up a health insurance plan. I was making big bucks, a handful of coins at a time.

We had supply space in one of the office buildings where vendors delivered dairy, pastries, bagels, coffee and espresso both fresh-roasted. I confess I did the trips to Ghirardelli Chocolate on my own to purchase twenty-pound cases of powdered chocolate. While there, I bought treats for my workers. And myself, of course. We made the best mochas in the city, bar none. Before I was done, Wayne's Brews began to cater event locations, and I even opened storefront coffee shops.

One evening I went to Lone Star with Glenda and Sarah. We were celebrating the success I was having with catering, and we were enjoying ourselves. I noticed a young man watching us from the sidelines, and asked if he wanted to join. Conversation rolled along between three old friends, and we made that shy newcomer feel at home. Ed joined us for dinner in the Castro. He was a computer artist, and the rest of us didn't even know what that was at the time. He fascinated us all. As he opened up, he teased us as luddites, and we him as a geek.

Ed and I dated for several weeks before he moved in. I knew he'd never be a replacement for Joe in my heart, but he was energetic, fun, and open to assimilating my lifestyle. He displayed some of his art at one of my coffee carts; the owner of a computer company saw his work, and hired Ed to join his team of artists. For a while there, I was quite the hero!

After two years together, Ed and I split ways. He was honest enough to tell me he wanted other men, not me alone. I think he was surprised that I told him it was all or nothing; it's not the answer he wanted. Ed's new bear friend helped him move out of my apartment and into his. Two weeks later, that friend kicked Ed out, too ... that bear didn't want an open relationship either.

Ed's biggest gift to me was, oddly enough, his mother. I adored her. Elaine knew he was gay and liked me over any of his earlier partners. She hoped we would settle into a permanent situation. The three of us had dinner together monthly. Elaine suffered from what was then called Multiple Personality Disorder, so Ed and I were never sure just who would show up.

It tickled me until I learned just how dreadful her background had been. Ghastly abuse led her to such severe dissociation. She told me once that to her, a gay man was a safe man; I'm happy I could fill that role for her. She had good counseling and is one of the lucky ones who developed a degree of control over her inner selves. Elaine is still my friend. Because we talk now and then, I know her son is doing well but living alone. Ed was not geared to be a one and only.

The next man to catch my eye caused me to break my own rule about being careful. Shaun was my idea of super-hot, a powerfully-built knockout who could have modeled as a mountain man. I'd seen him often enough in the Castro but stayed away; each time he was with a different man. Nonetheless, when the day came that he flashed that big smile at me, I was as helpless as those fainting gals in the romance novels.

We spent the afternoon having sex in his apartment. His body, under the hair, was hard, smooth, and limber. His erection appeared to be a permanent fixture, as ready for action as an automatic rifle. In the gay world, there are tops and bottoms. I am a top. Shaun was ... well, you get the idea. As I dressed late in the day, untangling my clothes from his sheets, he told me he was soon going back to Texas to see his boyfriend.

Well, shit.

Shaun was everything I warned myself against. It took a real chump to go anywhere near him. But I'd done it anyway. It was time I got out of the gay lifestyle of the city by the bay. There was nothing but trouble there for me.

It was time to make some changes with Wayne's Brews, too. Starbucks was moving into San Francisco. This was extreme good fortune for me because the company bought the equipment I had in my storefront locations. I kept looking for a loophole as I stuffed my pockets with money and got out of town. This was a happier exit than most of my life chapters had been.

The last time I'd seen Seattle was with Winkie, when I was a poor married man. I decided to take another look at the Emerald City with enough freedom and funds to enjoy it.

15.

Great Expectations

I liked Seattle when Winkie and I visited on our honeymoon, some three decades earlier. The drive up the coast through Oregon to Washington is gorgeous, a twisty two-lanes through forests and along Pacific beaches. The further north you go, the more the Northwest envelops you with wide arms of evergreen, snowy peaks, and inlets cutting in from the sea. I somehow felt *wanted* as I drew near. Of course, this same land is home to the Sasquatch, so not all of its lures are equally charming.

As I drove, I thought about my admittedly slutty behavior with Shaun. A handsome man, for sure. Young and buff. Sexy as hell. But a player, and I knew it. For a man like me seeking a permanent partner, Shaun was a trip into Crazyville. Why had I thrown aside all my rules of conduct in order to bed him?

I guess astounding sex outdistances almost anything else in life. Nothing feels real in the moment except the moment. Or maybe I couldn't find my one perfect partner because I wasn't projecting the image that I wanted one. If that was the case, the problem wasn't the San Francisco lifestyle; it was me.

What did I know about perfection anyway? Mama the Whore and Daddy the Absent weren't shining examples. The Mormons didn't understand the concept, not in my case anyway. The closest to perfection that I ever came was my very first relationship. I was sixteen when James entered my life and swept me off my feet. Sure, I needed a daddy figure. Sure, I was naive. Despite that frown of disapproval I see on your face, I never felt used or manipulated by him (I don't believe Joe ever felt used by me, when I was the older man in the couple). It's possible I've just forgotten, or I never recognized it because I had so much pent-up love to release. At the end of the day, I'm not sure how much of what you don't remember actually matters. I needed a pure memory more than I needed a pure truth.

James and I connected in every way. For four years I had a glimpse of the finest that love has to offer. And yet, I left James to go to Paris. How did a kid make such a tough decision? Why not cancel my plan?

I've grappled with that, trying to understand. I had a solitary goal that was my only beacon of hope. I could not merely cast it aside. That Paris dream was the only thing I had to lift me out of squalor. I'd held it tight for so long. I actually believed our relationship would transcend my years in school. I may never have gone if I had known Paris would put an end to James and me. I'd searched for him ever since, but he had disappeared for good. I'd always sought a relationship to eclipse the one with him, but I was giving up on the idea that it would ever happen. A psychiatrist might have other answers, but these are the ones that make sense to me.

I rented an apartment in West Seattle, which is south of the main city on Puget Sound. The California boy in me, now encased in a fifty-something man, liked living close to a beach. Alki qualified, even though rain was more likely than sun. I lived there for a few months and took a part-time job in a bagel shop. The owner was terrible with people, capable of failing in a boom economy, but I really didn't care; I just wanted a place to be that would keep me busy. Money was no longer an issue, after the sale of my coffee empire. In fact, when I bought a Toyota pickup ... because everybody in Washington State drove a pickup ... the dealer said I must have gold balls. He'd never seen a higher credit score.

Seattle was flexing its muscle in the 1990s, experiencing a sometimes painful growth spurt. Microsoft was the place to work, dotcoms flourished, Amazon was just a quirky bookseller. Music was exploding, fabulous restaurants popped up like mushrooms, and rent was still cheap. Seattle could barely contain its own energy. But when it came to gay men, it was a mini San Francisco. Everybody was looking for one-night stands.

Except me. I joined the Bear Club in Seattle and attended lots of their events (I was even voted Mr. Northwest Bear at one of them). But it was for camaraderie, not commitment.

I was probably undermining myself. For me there was no midpoint. It was either a totally perfect relationship, or a totally imperfect one like the wild time with Shaun . Given time, he would have burned me to be sure, but he was stuck in my craw.

Then one day, his letter arrived. He bemoaned how much he wished he'd never left. Shaun exuded sex and charm and sorrow over his past trespasses. He wanted a chance to give monogamy a try.

Should I have said no? Of course.

Could I trust him? Of course not.

Did I have the potential to be an idiot? Well, at least my dick did. It convinced me that Shaun was the cure for my loneliness. Why not at least see him. I couldn't feel much worse, right? And maybe Shaun would keep his word. A life lesson: no man should listen to his dick when it quits consulting his brain.

I let my bad boy move in with me, establishing only two rules: No other men and no drugs.

"No worries," Shaun said. He soon found a job with a company that sold and installed lighting. I knew for a fact he'd mastered the art of lighting up a bedroom.

I should never have tried to change the scoundrel, but I thought with my guidance he would see all the benefits to commitment. We started looking for a place to buy in Seattle or the surrounding towns. Shaun claimed to have money from an insurance policy that a dead boyfriend left him, so we could share the costs.

We took state ferries to places like Vashon Island, Winslow on Bainbridge Island, and finally to the Olympic Peninsula. The further west, the wilder the country, pockmarked here and there by small, often artistic communities. I found property west of Port Angeles that I loved; it was evergreen forest on a cliff overlooking the Strait of Juan de Fuca. *We could build on it,* I thought. But I immediately reconsidered. I wanted to trust the beautiful, carefree Shaun, but I didn't really know if he'd stay with me long enough to build a house.

Heading back toward Kingston to catch a ferry home, I saw a sign to Port Townsend. A Realtor had told me, "Oh you don't want to go there. It's full of hippies." I turned off the highway. My life in Venice Beach on the boardwalk had more than prepared me for a hippie lifestyle. As soon as I pulled into town I was in love. I bought a three-bedroom, two-bath house in a scenic, serene area that backed up to Fort Worden.

I admit I bought it for me, not for us. Shaun was not the least interested in scenery or serenity. He wanted grunge bands and body heat. What the hell was I thinking? He kept his job in Seattle, making the effort to commute from Port Townsend. On weekends he flew to San Francisco to continue a gig as a DJ there.

One day, he came home and put a sheet of paper in the freezer. I pulled it out and saw pink dots all over it.

"What is this?" I asked.

"Drugs," he said.

I had no idea what it was, but I walked to the den and threw it into the flames burning in our fireplace.

"What the fuck?" Shaun shrieked.

"No drugs!" I replied. "That was our agreement."

Our days as a couple were numbered.

I discovered Shaun 's affair because he left an email open on the computer where I could see it. Intentional? Maybe. He was writing to a friend about a guy he'd met in Seattle. He was going to the guy's house when he told me he was working late. About the same time, one of my friends in San Francisco sent me an email, attaching a photo of Shaun and another man.

When he got home, I told him to pack up and leave. I didn't confront him about what he'd been doing; I was afraid I would lose my temper and knock him out. I sold him the Toyota pickup, and he left for San Francisco. By the way? I never saw any of that insurance money he had inherited. I was not surprised by Shaun's deception, nor was my sorrow very deep. Mostly, I felt a fool for settling on a false relationship. It was time to work on my self-respect.

Sometimes, when you're feeling crappy, only a puppy will do. I noticed people gathered around a pickup truck at a gas station. When I took a look, my heart did a complex gymnastic routine of joy. The truck bed held six black lab pups.

"How much?" I asked immediately.

"Free to good homes," said the lady.

I reached into the squirmy pile of babies. One licked my hand.

"Looks like she chooses you," the woman said.

I named the pup Maxine. She brought pure love into my life for many years. In fact, after Shaun moved out and Maxine moved in, I started painting again. I did canvases of the lighthouse near Fort Worden, of the waterfront, and of the old Victorian buildings that give Port Townsend its personality. My little town was quite the bustling commerce center in the early 1800s. It's easy to imagine a dozen steamships in the harbor, unloading and loading international goods.

When I felt a touch of boredom, I applied for a part-time job at a coffee shop. The owner was intimidated by my background in the business. It's the only time in my life I was rejected due to over-qualification. While I was walking back to my car, I saw a Help Wanted sign in a lovely shop window. The gallery was called Great Expectations. It was owned by a lady whose name was, no kidding, Merry.

Merry hired me on the spot. Within a few days, she asked me to work full-time, giving me keys to the shop so I could open in the morning. Great Expectations was a dream job. It had a tremendous inventory of unique gifts. I loved colored clear glass, especially blue. Merry sold me blue rabbits, birds, and bottles of every size and shape. She also sold copper pots and pans, and I loaded up like I was mining the metal. I still have twelve copper pots and buckets hanging in my kitchen over the center cook top island. They've never been used, but wow, are they gorgeous.

I bought an entire village of Department 56 Christmas homes, shops, boats, and lighthouse. Today, they are on the ledge overlooking the front room in the loft on the third floor. They have lights inside that I turn on during the holidays. I was taking so much stuff home that I gave most of my paycheck back to Merry.

Merry allowed me to sell my paintings in her shop. Life fit again. Time passed, months into years. I didn't give up on finding Mr. Right but I knew it was a long shot. There were other things in life to build my joy around. I was still a member of the Bears Club in Seattle so I would go now and then for an infusion of that lifestyle. But frankly, I was mostly a tourist there.

On one trip to the Bears Club, I met a man who worked for a gay publication. He was interested in Port Townsend and asked if I would pose for him.

"NOT NUDE!!!" I huffed.

"I just want shots around town," he replied, taken aback.

It turned out to be fun. I posed in my PT baseball cap for photos in the town's beauty spots. I didn't subscribe to the magazine, but the photographer mailed me a copy of the issue I was in. I thoroughly enjoyed it.

The article and its photos had a fortuitous consequence. A North Carolina man began an email correspondence with me. We exchanged photos of ourselves, our homes, our dogs. It was nice, getting to know a person before meeting him. I'd never done that before. John had family in the area and wrote he might stop by one day. He liked the look of Port Townsend and, I presume, of me.

At Merry's shop, I met a gay couple who lived a few blocks away from me. They told me that there was a weekly lunch meeting of several gay people. I attended some and even celebrated my sixtieth birthday with them. My social life was expanding, and I went to Seattle less and less, feeling content right where I was.

Content.

That may be as much as we can truly hope for. Maxine was my shadow at home. She'd sit with me while I painted some of the best work of my life. When a football game was on, nobody told me to turn it down. Adventure novels were a passion of mine. I'd build a fire and read for hours with classical music playing on the stereo. Often I fell asleep to awake in the middle of the night, the fire out and the house getting cold. I'd go to bed.

Merry and I became close. Her sister and daughter worked at Great Expectations, and her mother would stop by frequently. I was surprised how many different languages I heard while working there. Sometimes people came in speaking French. It was fun to listen to them, and they were surprised when I commented to them in French.

Content.

In January 1998, a handsome man walked into the shop. Merry turned to greet him, but I told her I would take care of this customer.

"How can I help you?" I asked the man, smiling. I felt suddenly shy. For the love of God, I was sixty-years-old and yet a blush heated my neck and cheeks.

He grinned back at me. "I'm just looking around." And he stared at me.

"Are you stalking me?" I asked.

"Yes. I think I am."

This was North Carolina John. We recognized each other from the photos we'd shared as we exchanged emails. He'd said he would come by, but I didn't know when.

Normally, Merry and I went to one of the shops, picked up food, and brought it back for lunch. Today, I asked John out. Merry looked at us, then told me to take as long as I wanted. She admitted later she knew that very second that I'd found my perfect man. "The chemistry nearly burned the old place down!"

There was a cafe next door. After lunch, I went back in the shop and asked Merry if I could take the rest of the day off. John and I toured Port Townsend. That was the last day I worked at the store called Great Expectations. From then on, I started living them.

16.

Life with John

At long last I get to tell you a love story that does not end in tragedy. It lives on into its third decade.

We knew so much about each other through correspondence by the time we met, that John and I were already half in love. We beamed through that first lunch. John was a retired school teacher with a master's degree in marine biology. He'd taught in California and then Florida at a nature center. After touring Port Townsend, we took a short trip to Oregon, the first of many journeys we were to make with one another.

From the very beginning we clicked. John was a bicyclist. He'd been a member of a racing team, and still kept his body in perfect shape. He lived part of his life in Florida, so he was nearly permanently tanned, with enough dark hair here and there to captivate a bear like me. I found him seriously attractive. Like many relationships, it started there. But the more time we spent together the more he surprised me with likes similar to my own. He was a builder, and I knew a lot about rehabbing. We loved watching movies, reading thrillers, talking politics. Thank goodness we both belonged to the same political party. It was as if I were in a spell … all I knew was that I wanted to be with this man.

John's dog showed far more reserve about me. Buster had been beaten repeatedly before John rescued him, and he never quite forgave most humans, although he liked Maxine. He terrified me. Nonetheless, Buster became my collateral. John received a call that he was needed in Florida. Would he return? He promised he'd come back to me as soon as possible. He left Buster and his truck in my care, so I assumed he was serious about our relationship. I far preferred the truck to the dog.

John called from Florida to tell me he'd put his house there up for sale and made arrangements to ship his boat to Washington. On his next call, he asked me to meet him at John Wayne airport in Orange County, California. "John Wayne" tickled us; we liked having something named after both of us.

I found an intrepid kennel to take the dogs; fortunately Buster the white Samoyed and Maxine the black Labrador got along famously. Merry drove me to the dock in Kingston to catch a ferry to Edmonds, then a van to SeaTac. "Adios, you lucky man," she said with a hug. " I expect you to continue being my best customer."

John was in Orange County to meet me when I arrived. My emotions cavorted; I felt like I hadn't seen him in months.

The next weeks of our lives were spent touring old haunts like Venice Beach. My family shack was long gone and so was my ghost; I believe James could finally say goodbye to me as I walked the same beach with a different love. I saw where John (a California boy like me) grew up, and we went to Colorado so he could meet my sister, Jacquie. On a whim, we drove to North Carolina so I could see his property there, then on to Florida, and back to Washington to pick up the dogs.

From the day we met, I knew life could be a lot better than *content*. On January 8, 2008, we became Domestic Partners, Washington State's answer to gay marriage. We'd been "living in sin" for nine lusty, lucky years by then; we decided we'd go for a record so we're still at it.

Memories from the past two decades with John come at me a bit like birdshot. So here is a scattering for you:

REAL ESTATE

John loved to buy and sell houses. We still have properties in California, North Carolina, and Washington. He was always a hard worker, and so was I. The physical work of rehabbing homes kept us both in greati shape.

To travel from one holding to another, we took many road trips. On long hauls, we'd belt out the old standards I learned with my Gramma at community sings. His big truck bounced down the highway to the strains of *Polly Wooly Doodle* and *High Hopes*, then on through folk, disco and rock. In the back seat, Maxine grinned and Buster mumbled at the sound of my voice landing between the keys.

In Crumpler, NC, John showed me his own home. I saw right away why he loved that gorgeous country. The tiny town contained a post office, a hardware store, a beauty shop, and a market. All in one building. The surrounding hills were lush, and a river flowed through the valley. His house sat on top of a hill overlooking all the beauty. I was busy taking photos of everything I wanted to oil paint.

I was surprised when John stopped the car abruptly. When I turned, I saw a farmer in the road ahead of us. John lowered his window, and as the leathery old beanpole walked up to us, it was easy to see he was angry. He didn't greet John but opened with a growl. "Did you know niggers bought the house across the road from you?"

John started rolling his window back up.

The farmer asked, "Whadda ya gonna do?"

John said, "Go up the hill to greet our new neighbors."

I was temporarily speechless. I'd never heard that kind of hate in the black neighborhood where I grew up. In Venice Beach, we were all poor together. Without the help of my friend Clarence's family, a white woman and her two scrawny kids would have missed a lot more meals than we did.

As we continued up the hill, John warned me, "We have to be careful. If the neighbors knew we were gay, they'd burn the house down."

This was my introduction to life in the South.

John's house had a beautiful location but it was moldering away. His bathroom had not been hooked up to a drain for the toilet. The shower and the sink worked, but to use a toilet for its intended purpose, you had to go downstairs and walk to the back of the A-frame. I was surprised at its condition. John could envision almost anything, but was content living like he had almost nothing. He said he feared break-ins when he was gone for long periods if the property appeared too attractive.

We stayed in Crumpler a couple of days then took off for Florida. His West Palm Beach home was a whole different story. The house was beautiful, spacious and pristine with a glorious swimming pool in the backyard, protected by a screened enclosure. But I didn't like the Florida heat, and it activated my asthma.

On the return trip from Florida to Port Townsend, John talked about selling the house in Florida and buying a new house in Washington.

"But why?" I loved my home.

"It's such a little house."

"Three bedrooms? Two baths? Den with fireplace? We talking about the same place?"

"But no double office or billiard room or media center."

"Big yard the dogs love? Backs up on forest?"

"But nowhere near enough room for the polo ponies."

I caved. We sold the Florida house and my "little" house, combining funds to find the Washington residence that suited us both. Something with good bones but that would allow us to exercise our joy in construction and rehabilitation.

GAY BASHING

Because I spent most of my life in Paris, Washington, and California, I had a skewed view of the attitudes toward gay people. I'd lived through the fear of it being illegal to the joy of gay parades. I was unprepared for North Carolina.

John assured me it wasn't funny, that homosexuals kept their lifestyle to themselves.

"We're back in the closet as long as we're here?" I huffed.

"So far back we'll need lanterns to find our way out."

I believed him, sort of. I believed him for sure when I had an experience of my own. We were rehabbing a beautiful riverside home near Winston-Salem. I'd been painting an attached screened porch and discovered mold on the ceiling. Wearing a mask, I brushed on a mold cleaner. All of a sudden I could not catch my breath. I found John in the house and let him know I couldn't breathe freely. He loaded me into the truck and headed to the nearest emergency room.

John told them what had happened. Hospital orderlies wheeled me away, and the first round of medical experts determined I was in Afib (Atrial fibrillation). I was hooked to an EKG and wired to an intravenous line. All the while, I tried to tell them I knew about the Afib, but this was an asthma attack. Asthma had always plagued me. Finally, they treated me for the asthma, but the emergency doctor still wanted to put me into the Cardiac Care Unit.

I told him I had a friend in the waiting room and asked if he could come in.

"Is he related to you?" he asked.

"Yes. He's my husband."

The room plunged into a deep freeze. Two nurses marched out.

"We don't treat your kind here," the doc said. "Go back to Washington to find a doctor there." Then he left the room.

Nobody came back. They'd given me a diuretic, and I had to piss, so I rang the nurse to ask for a urinal. No response. I rang again. No response. I pulled off the leads to the EKG and heard the alarm go off down the hall. Still nobody came. Finally, I struggled up. The only thing I had on was a hospital gown so I peed on the floor. I pulled the intravenous line out of my arm, so gay blood joined gay urine on their floor. I found my clothes and started putting them on.

Finally the doctor came back, viewed the wreckage, and silently put a bandage on my arm then wheeled me to the lobby.

John saw me and scurried over. I told him through tight lips that we were leaving. In the car, I recounted the whole thing. He wanted to go back and spread around a little more blood, but I said I needed to get home fast to see my doctor.

Laura picked me up at the airport and drove me to the hospital in Port Angeles. My doctor ran tests and said my heart was doing fine, that it was a bad case of asthma due to the mold cleaner no doubt.

After that, I lost interest in visiting North Carolina. It is a gorgeous state with many fine people. But they weren't on duty when I needed them. Bottom line, I can't change how people feel about me, any more than I can change the way I am. It's their craziness, not mine. I wish I'd realized that as a much younger man; it would have made so much difference.

ABOUT THE DOGS

Buster the Wicked and Maxine the Sweet stayed with us until they couldn't any more. Buster never changed much. He bit me once so badly, I had stitches on the back of my hand. If he was in the car, he refused to let me in unless John was with me.

With John giving us both orders of conduct, the Samoyed finally realized that I was going to be around, like the family black sheep. He accepted me with very little grace, often mumbling low to himself. Meanwhile, he taught Maxine to quit being pleasant to the other pooches in the dog park. And he was relegated to the garage whenever we had guests so he wouldn't nip the backs of their legs just for the sport of it.

Buster avoided the rainbow bridge, instead taking the highway to hell when his time came. Since then, John and I have continued to adopt rescues of a more obliging nature.

OUR WASHINGTON HOME

After the hospital fiasco, John agreed that North Carolina was not the best place for us to call our permanent home. We returned to Port Townsend. After the sales of my home and his in Florida, we had ample funds for a mini-mansion, one with great views and more space. We looked at several in Jefferson County, then Clallam County.

In 1999, we found our forever home. It was love at first look. The couple selling it was also gay; we laughed at the idea of keeping it in the family. It is three stories with a view of Sequim Bay, John Wayne Marina (because of its name, we tell friends it's our marina), and the Strait of Juan de Fuca. We can see the lights at night from Victoria, Canada. The lot is five acres with great trails through the cedar and fir. The Olympic mountains are visible to the south. If you can put up with rain, fog, and slugs, this place is paradise on earth.

John had his 32-foot Gaff Cutter moved to the north. In dry dock, we sanded the bottom, sealed any cracks, and painted it with a special nautical paint to protect it from salt water and barnacles. Eventually, we rented a slip for the sailboat in the John Wayne Marina.

BELIEF IS BACK

One day I drove to Sequim for a haircut. I met another customer who'd been reading a book on managing people. We chatted, and when the barber called my name, this stranger handed me his card. He invited me to visit his church.

I thought he was just a member of a congregation who wanted to share an experience that he enjoyed. But when I went, it turned out he was the pastor. I sat in the back to observe, and I was touched by his sermon as well as his rapport with his congregation. He had a great sense of humor and a real understanding of his message. This wasn't a Mormon church. And I liked it.

When I went to my car afterwards, I noticed an old barn a short distance from the parking lot, across a field of lavender. The morning sky was alive with white puffs dotting the blue. It was a lovely sight, so I took pictures of it. As I got in my car, the pastor came over and asked me to come again.

I doubted I would. Religion had seared me with enough scars. I wasn't eager to give it another go at me. But those photos prompted me to paint a canvas of that old barn. I had a lot of time to think about that day, watching a congregation happy with their minister and each other. When I completed the painting, I made a print for the Pastor, had it framed, and took it to him one Sunday morning. I stayed for the service and enjoyed the subject of his sermon.

The following week I returned. Before the service, the Pastor took me to his office and showed me he'd hung the painting in a place of honor. He loved it. I was beginning to feel like a feral cat, finally accepting food from the hand of a cajoling human. Was this guy for real? Could he replace Bishop Gregory in my life for guidance and friendship?

The next Sunday, as the congregation shook hands with the pastor after the service, I overheard him ask the man ahead of me how teaching French was going. That piqued my interest. Then the pastor asked him how his husband was doing.

In French, I exclaimed aloud, telling the man I had a husband, too.

After that, the pastor and I went to his office. He listened intently as I shared with him that I had been a Mormon, and they had excommunicated me from the church. He told me that being homosexual was okay as far as his congregation and he were concerned. He asked me to join. "You won't be the only one, I assure you," he said.

"But Pastor, I've been excommunicated. I can't take the Sacrament when offered."

"Wayne, you're not in the Mormon Church anymore. In this house, you are welcome." The next Sunday he gave an outstanding sermon about Jesus accepting everyone into his flock.

On Sunday mornings, I go to the Lutheran Church. I'm a member now. John cycles trails in a nearby park. We meet up afterwards to go to breakfast. Our needs are fed. My son Doug, a devout Mormon, told me it was appropriate I was a Lutheran, since I was a rebel. I don't think I rebelled so much as I was dumped. Whatever truth you choose, this "rebel" has found his home.

MY FAMILY

This story is mine, not theirs, so I have not shared many family secrets. But it has not always been free from hurt and blame.

My daughter lives just down the main road in Sequim. She moved here when her husband became abusive to her, and she was worried for her children. It has been a constant pleasure for me to have them so close to home.

My twin sons are both important members of their Mormon congregations, one in Washington and the other in California. As kids, they were raised by their mother and resented what I had done to explode the family. Today, they each grapple with accepting my lifestyle, one with greater success than the other.

My sister Jacquie lives in Colorado. She did become a fifth wife to the man she followed to Mexico. He set up different households for each family. Jacquie was widowed a long time ago. We still talk often, and I am eternally grateful that I had this one fierce supporter throughout my life.

Winkie is the hardest to talk about. She still lives in San Bernardino, in fact in the same house we had when we were married. She never remarried, and our three children moved away from that community. I've seen her only once when one of my sons thought we could meet. He brought her to my house. She never even spoke to me, so I'd have to say the flames of hate still burned bright within. I've asked forgiveness and been denied. I'm afraid that trail has come to an end. I hope she has found happiness within her circle of Mormon friends.

MR. RIGHT

John and I have been together for over twenty years. Like any couple we have our moments of disagreement. That's part of life between two men, each of whom has a dominant streak. But neither of us needs to be king. We allow for individuality.

We are passionately in love. Together, we still manage real estate. And we support each other in our separate endeavors. I am an artist and spend hours painting in oil, listening to classical music. John is a cycling enthusiast and also spends hours riding and building bikes, listening to his rock music.

John knows the pain the Mormon Church caused me, and with his loving care, a lot of the anger has finally slipped away. He is happy I have found a new church. We keep each other young by growing old together.

17.

Everything I Ever Wanted

When I was growing up in the ghetto of Venice Beach, poverty was a constant. We didn't always have food. We used pages from the Sears catalog to wipe our butts. Head lice were frequent houseguests. Jacquie and I walked when other families drove. The house was lit by one bulb in a dangerous socket. Why we didn't burst into flames, I'll never know.

I lived in the shack for twelve years. I wanted out of that kind of squalor, and I have achieved that. I am not cold or hungry or living in foulness.

I was desperate to feel good about myself. My aching need for affection had one good result, I think; it caused me to help others if for no other reason than they would like me. I folded papers for the other paperboys, I was a reasonable boss, I supported the concierge in Paris, I worked with AIDS victims making their last days better. I always gave more money than was asked by the Mormon Church. I donate to the homeless and volunteer at soup kitchens. Maybe these things count in my favor when I am assessed for the harm I did Winkie.

I'm no Goodie Two Shoes; I can be petty, biting, cynical. But I've come to accept who I am today, partly through the writing of this book. The process of reexamination has helped me find peace.

Even as a youngster, I had feelings for other boys. I knew I was different. And it was dangerous. I had to hide any emotion. Fear was a constant companion for James and me. Arrest could have separated us at any time.

My country has become more tolerant of gays during my lifetime. Even accepting my experience in North Carolina, I have found whole communities of "my kind." I am not so different after all.

I wanted a religion that cherished me and made me strong in my beliefs; instead I received Gay Aversion Therapy. In the end, I knew the Mormon Church was wrong to cajole me into marriage with a woman. The "only true church" on the planet lied when they told me it would cure my gayness. It is also not free from blame in the pain borne by Winkie.

From my earliest days, I've looked for the love first denied by uncaring parents. The search was frustrated by disillusionment, loss, and so much sorrow. Just as I was about to give up on it, John came along. As we have both gotten older, my role has changed to caregiver. John was bitten by a tick in North Carolina recently and now has Lyme disease. His memory slips more all the time. As for me, my heart condition is not getting any better. I'm not looking forward to last days, but I will do whatever needs done for us both.

I wish I could return through the years to comfort that terrified young boy, riddled with pain after the rape by his mother's trick. I would hold that boy, praise him, and assure him he was exactly as he should be. All would be well. I would tell him he would become a proud gay man. He would not be alone or in want. He would be a good person and have a good life. His goals would be met.

I have lived and loved well. What more can anyone want from their life?

Acknowledgments

I am grateful to Linda B. Myers for helping me look into some very dark corners of my past. Without her diligence, I could not have brought this story together.

Heidi Hansen of OlyPen Books and cover designer Roslyn McFarland of Far Lands Publishing together created the handsome book you are holding in your hands.

I am profoundly grateful for the strong support of my sister Jacquie. Everybody should have a big sister to help fight their battles.

I am sorry for the times my actions and beliefs caused my family stress, and I rejoice that my children are all in my life, allowing me to share theirs.

My husband John is a shining light that steadies me; finding him makes my journey worth all the potholes and detours. Now that we're entering our third decade together, I think this marriage is going to take.

I rejoice that my dear friend Glenda still calls if only to laugh with me. The photo on the back cover of this book is one she took of John and me.

I celebrate a teacher who saw a spark of talent in a troubled child. A cafe owner who kept an eye out for a newspaper boy alone in the dark. A postmistress who didn't question an obviously fake ID. A French professor who thought I was worth the colorful paints. A concierge who loved an American despite herself. All the coffee freaks who built me a tiny empire. Beautiful, bright men I have known who don't accept there is anything wrong with the way they live and love.

There are many compassionate people I respected when I was a Mormon. My issues with the Mormon Church have not often been with the Mormon people. I hope the Church will find its way to a different approach to homosexuality; until then, I am grateful that so many others are opening their doors.